"There is great help in this new book by Don and Doug. It reveals clues on how God 'mysteriously and marvelously' moves people toward himself. I'm incorporating the content into my teaching, starting *today*."

LON ALLISON, DIRECTOR, BILLY GRAHAM CENTER, WHEATON COLLEGE, AND COAUTHOR OF *GOING PUBLIC WITH THE GOSPEL*

"Of the many books on the practice of evangelism this is one that does not leave the reader feeling frustrated and guilty! It does not promote an engineered confrontation but invites us to build respectful relationships and engage in stimulating conversation."

EDDIE GIBBS, SENIOR PROFESSOR OF CHURCH GROWTH, FULLER THEOLOGICAL SEMINARY, AUTHOR OF *CHURCHNEXT* AND *LEADERSHIPNEXT*

"When it comes to evangelism, a one-size-fits-all approach has not worked for a long time—if ever. Schaupp and Everts have helped us all by actually finding out how students these days are making their way to faith. The view of evangelism that emerges is relational, natural and full of integrity."

STEPHEN A. HAYNER, PROFESSOR OF EVANGELISM, COLUMBIA THEOLOGICAL SEMINARY

"This book starts and ends on the ground, just where most of us need help in sharing our faith. It coaches us in practical ways to both discern and respond to where people really are. Its prolific examples amplify and apply very important values that are embedded in the gospel, alongside those that are features of our postmodern cultural life. This is a very motivating and useful book, and I commend it enthusiastically."

MARK LABBERTON, SENIOR PASTOR, FIRST PRESBYTERIAN CHURCH OF BERKELEY, AND AUTHOR OF *THE DANGEROUS ACT OF WORSHIP*

"Doug and Don have looked into the mystery of postmodern conversion and given us some handles and helps so that we can serve people well in their spiritual journey toward Christ. I am very excited about their keen insight and practical approach, and am recommending the book to many."

RICK RICHARDSON, ASSOCIATE PROFESSOR AND DIRECTOR, M.A. IN EVANGELISM AND LEADERSHIP PROGRAM, WHEATON COLLEGE GRADUATE SCHOOL, AND AUTHOR OF *REIMAGINING EVANGELISM* AND *EVANGELISM OUTSIDE THE BOX*

"*I Once Was Lost* is an enormous gift to the church. Schaupp and Everts show us a clear (yet neither facile nor simplistic) vision of the path to postmodern conversion. Individually, conversion is grounded in the mysteries of God working in lives. Collectively, a discernible pattern exists. This is an extraordinary book."

MARTHA GRACE REESE, AUTHOR OF *UNBINDING THE GOSPEL* AND THE REAL LIFE EVANGELISM SERIES

"Set in the very heart of today's culture, *I Once Was Lost* brings to light the contours of the conversion experience for real people in real life. Moreover, Don Everts and Doug Schaupp peer beyond mere description, prescribing practical and specific guidance for ushering skeptical seekers across the threshold into the kingdom. This illuminating resource tool will most certainly inspire within you and your small group a heart and a pathway for reaching the lost."

GARRY POOLE, DIRECTOR OF EVANGELISM, WILLOW CREEK COMMUNITY CHURCH, AND AUTHOR OF *SEEKER SMALL GROUPS*

"I am so excited about this book! . . . After just a few minutes of reading it I felt inspired and more equipped to articulate my faith."

TOMMY WALKER, SONGWRITER AND WORSHIP LEADER

"Doug and Don and their brothers and sisters with InterVarsity have discerned a new movement of God's Spirit among our post-Christian, postmodern culture. Their insights from the frontlines of campus ministry provide a whole new paradigm for viewing the process by which one becomes a member of the kingdom of God."

DOUGLAS SCOTT, WRITER AND FILMMAKER, CREATIVE CATALYST AND VIDEO PRODUCER, WILLOW CREEK COMMUNITY CHURCH

"Doug and Don bring us right back to what it was like to be 'lost.' Holding the delicate balance between mystery and analysis, this contribution to the discussion of conversion is invaluable and will undoubtedly lead to more effective and organic ministry for all who put it into practice. This book is a must-read for those seeking to make an eternal difference in the lives of non-Christians today."

YORK MOORE, EVANGELIST AND AUTHOR OF *GROWING YOUR FAITH BY GIVING IT AWAY*

"In *I Once Was Lost,* Don Everts and Doug Schaupp do a masterful job helping us discover how to be a guide alongside of our friends. Through the complex lives and winsome stories of their friends, Don and Doug help us to better understand the journey to faith and the thresholds that need to be crossed to become followers of Jesus."

JIMMY LONG, AUTHOR OF *EMERGING HOPE* AND THE *EMERGING CULTURE CURRICULUM KIT*

"What's in the secret sauce? It took two decades of lab work to find out, but two campus ministers working two different kitchens have picked up the five pivotal 'thresholds' that usher postmoderns into faith. This will be high on my list of the most important books on evangelism published so far in the twenty-first century."

LEONARD SWEET, DREW THEOLOGICAL SCHOOL, GEORGE FOX UNIVERSITY, WWW.SERMONS.COM

DON EVERTS
AND DOUG SCHAUPP

I ONCE WAS LOST

What Postmodern Skeptics Taught Us
About Their Path to Jesus

IVP Books

An imprint of InterVarsity Press
Downers Grove, Illinois

InterVarsity Press
P.O. Box 1400, Downers Grove, IL 60515-1426
World Wide Web: www.ivpress.com
E-mail: email@ivpress.com

InterVarsity Press® is the book-publishing division of InterVarsity Christian Fellowship/USA®, a student movement active on campus at hundreds of universities, colleges and schools of nursing in the United States of America, and a member movement of the International Fellowship of Evangelical Students. For information about local and regional activities, write Public Relations Dept., InterVarsity Christian Fellowship/USA, 6400 Schroeder Rd., P.O. Box 7895, Madison, WI 53707-7895, or visit the IVCF website at <www.intervarsity.org>.

All Scripture quotations, unless otherwise indicated, are taken from the Holy Bible, Today's New International Version™ Copyright © 2001 by International Bible Society. All rights reserved.

Material from Maité Rodriguez on pp. 103-5 and 117-18 is used by permission of Maité Rodriguez. A fuller version of this story is told in John Teter, Get the Word Out (Downers Grove, Ill.: InterVarsity Press, 2003), pp. 63-67.

Design: Cindy Kiple
Images: Max Oppenheim/Getty Images

ISBN 978-0-8308-3608-6

Printed in the United States of America ∞

Library of Congress Cataloging-in-Publication Data

Everts, Don, 1971-
  I once was lost: what postmodern skeptics taught us about their
  path to Jesus / Don Everts and Doug Schaupp.
      p. cm.
  Includes bibliographical references and index.
  ISBN 978-0-8308-3608-6 (pbk.: alk. paper)
  1. Conversion—Christianity. 2. Postmodernism—Religious
  aspects—Christianity. 3. Witness bearing (Christianity) 4.
  Evangelistic work. I. Schaupp, Doug, 1967- II. Title.
  BT780.E94 2008
  248.2'4—dc22
                                                              2008002182

P   20   19   18   17   16   15   14   13   12   11   10   9
Y   24   23   22   21   20   19   18   17   16   15   14   13

We dedicate this book to Mailin Chu Young.

Mailin, this book would never have made it to print without your many hours of labor.

Thank you for your tireless writing assistance and your deep love for those who have never met Jesus.

Contents

Acknowledgments

It took a village to write this book. No joke.

Thank you to the amazing UCLA friends who first came up with this framework for understanding the process of coming to faith. And thank you to our InterVarsity staff friends who have tested, retested and dismantled the five thresholds over the past decade.

Thank you to those who encouraged this material to get to print in the first place. Thank you, Dr. Eddie Gibbs and Terry Erickson, for encouraging Mailin and me (Doug) in the initial phase of this project.

Thank you to those who gave us incredible input on the book. Your help, inspiration, encouragement and stories have made this book what it is. Thanks to Jon Ball, Brenda Chan, Lisa Corujo, Elizabeth English, Russell Fung, Matthew Graff, Erna Hackett, Jenny Hall, Serene Haughey, Steve Hayner, Al Hsu, Tom Hughes, Susan Johnson, Kelly Joiner, Ryan Pfeiffer, Abner Ramos, Sam Rizk, Maité Rodriguez-Caballero, Mark Stoleson, Alan Sun and Matt Taylor. John Teter, thank you for your help with the title.

And, finally, thanks to those who were a part of our own journeys to faith. Don thanks Ben Herr. Doug thanks Elias Gonzalez.

Meet the Authors
(All 2000 of Them!)

If you are a bit leery of anyone that claims to know anything conclusive about anything postmodern, then you are in good company. So are we.

The two of us have been ministering on the front lines of these confusing, mysterious cultural shifts since they became unmistakable in the early 1990s. And anytime someone has tried to define or clarify or label all these changes it has always seemed a bit cartoonish and naively overconfident to us.

The more sure the conclusions are about so-called postmodernity, the more incredulous we tend to become. If Microsoft Word still draws a red squiggly line underneath "postmodernity" we've figured it's still a bit too early to go jumping to conclusions. So we've just kept on ministering daily among college students, those who are riding the front waves of these inexorable, invisible shifts.[1]

Yet here we are, more than ten years later, attempting to say some-

---

[1]How do we define postmodernity? On the one hand, we know that we no longer live in the modern era of enlightenment confidence in human reason. On the other hand, we also know that the new emerging era is not yet clearly defined. So how do we define postmodernity? It's how things are right now. It's the in between times. We are more experiential than propositional in our connection to truth. We are more communal than individualistic. We value authenticity over theory. We understand struggle more than naive certainty. We are in process, and we will be different in ten or twenty years.

thing clear about postmodernity. Well, let's be specific: we are attempting to say something clear about postmodern conversions. And we don't feel that what we have to say is cartoonish or even naively conclusive. Find this hard to believe? We empathize. So before you toss this book aside as another misguided attempt to describe the indescribable, please allow us to explain ourselves.

OUR STORIES

Don Everts and Doug Schaupp here. We are both missionaries to the college campus in the United States. We labor inside a campus movement called InterVarsity Christian Fellowship that's been around these parts since the 1940s.

As members of this InterVarsity movement we walk alongside college students as they consider the world of faith in general and the revolution of Jesus in particular. Don has been at this since 1994 and is currently working with students and campus staff in Colorado. Doug has been at it even longer, laboring among students and staff in Los Angeles and various other cities in Southern California.

Doug: When the campus first entered the twilight zone of postmodernity, we knew we were in for a ride. In the early 1990s we could feel the tectonic plates shifting underneath us on campus. The students we worked with increasingly viewed the world around them in entirely different ways from what we were accustomed to. Though the tremors of change had been around for decades, the big "postmodern" shift became unavoidable in the 1990s. Students weren't responding in the same ways they had before. Sharing the truth of Jesus' gospel no longer moved people.

Our evangelistic labors resonated less, and had less fruit.

We were confronted with the tension of tough questions. How do we find our footing on this shifting terrain? How can we offer Jesus in this new milieu? How much are we willing to embrace and be changed by this seismic upheaval?

Tentatively at first, then with greater courage and resolve, we entered the new postmodern world. The 1990s became a decade of great experimentation and risk-taking as we learned to offer Jesus to the next generation. By 1995, we had jumped into the postmodern world with everything we had, no holds barred, no looking back. And what a ride it has been!

Within the campus ministry ranks of InterVarsity across the country many people began wrestling with these shifts on campus and how to respond to them. What do discipleship, evangelism, missions, Scripture study look like for these new students? As a movement we all experimented and prayed and failed and succeeded. It was the beginning of an exhilarating season.

Don: Most of my own labors have been on campuses in the Rocky Mountains. Cultural observers have often noted that new trends and shifts in the wider culture always seem to hit campus first, and I have found this to be true. They also observe that cultural shifts and movements begin on the two coasts and then make their way into the middle of the United States over time. I have found this to be true as well.

So while my staff and I were definitely feeling these cultural shifts in the 1990s, it always seemed that our colleagues on the coasts were being hit harder. And faster. In terms of evangelism, we were beginning to calmly ask questions, while Doug and his folks were having to experiment or die.

So over the years I decided to become a student of the coasts, to follow their experiments in evangelism and see what they were learning. This was how I ran into Doug and his friends. They were taking risks in evangelism and coming to some interesting conclusions about postmodern conversions. And while many of their attempts were intriguing in and of themselves, it was the fruit itself that held my gaze.

Doug and his staff never claimed to have found the silver bullet, but they were around hundreds of postmodern folks who were investigating the person of Jesus and becoming Christians. From 1996 to 2007, their region had seen more than twenty-two hundred considerably postmodern folks walk the path to faith in Jesus. The numbers caught my eye. But the stories were what caught my heart.

These were real students: Matthew and Abner and Mark and Susan . . . I met some of them and marveled at their stories. These students were becoming powerful believers—many of them becoming missionaries, pastors and evangelists. On more than thirty-six campuses in Southern California, both urban and suburban, the InterVarsity staff were surprised and delighted to begin seeing a higher percentage of conversions than most other regions of the country.

So when Doug and his fellow campus missionaries started telling their stories and writing down what they had been learning from these new believers about the postmodern path to faith, I leaned in. I wanted to hear what they had learned and were learning. And I am glad I did.

A SURPRISING CONSENSUS

While we encountered many wonderful books about postmodernity and even postmodern evangelism specifically, we became really interested in getting some real-life data about evangelism and conversion directly from the new postmodern context we walked and labored in day after day.

So we began talking with these new Christians about what happened to them. We talked with our own friends. We gathered staff from various campuses and heard their stories of students coming to faith in Jesus. We interviewed new Jesus followers and listened intently as they told us their stories. And during this process of curious (and pretty joyful!) investigation we began to detect some deep, overarching lessons from their collective experience.

To our initial surprise, we noticed certain common experiences among our friends' journeys to faith. As we celebrated all the conversions we had witnessed, the same themes were popping up again and again.

These general themes were so prevalent, in fact, that a group of us came up with what we started calling "the five thresholds" in an in-house working document that sought to give words to what we were seeing. This unpublished article began to circulate a bit. Then the news began to trickle back to us. Our friends around the United States and even in other parts of the world found these five phases to ring true for them in their own context.

We were stunned. Had these particular new believers actually taught us something generally true about the postmodern path to faith? The more confirmation we got as the years went on, the more we realized we were onto something real and true about conversion in this postmodern world.

For those of us who came up with these five thresholds in the first place, it feels a little like the TV commercial of the resilient Energizer bunny. No matter what that silly little bunny goes through, it just keeps on banging that drum. We actually expected the batteries of the five thresholds to die out within a few months. But nearly a decade later, the drum still beats.

In fact, a group of thirty of us gathered a few years ago for a conference to "kill the bunny." Our task was to poke holes in and dismantle the five thresholds with our latest stories of folks coming to faith in Jesus. After a rigorous day of discussion and debate, the five thresholds shocked us by emerging from the fray largely unscathed. The bunny was still alive and marching.

It would seem that all those new believers have taught us something. These real people had real conversion experiences. And their stories have taught us something real and true about the postmodern path to faith.

And here's the kicker: the more clearly we see the postmodern path to Jesus, the more natural and relevant and regular our witness becomes and the more fruit we see in evangelism. Understanding the postmodern path to faith is both freeing and empowering for those engaged in the kingdom task of evangelism.

Mark and Abner and the hundreds of others who have walked from the land of the lost into the kingdom of Jesus have steered us right. We take joy in their new lives and are indebted to them for their honest reflections on their spiritual travels. It's their consensus about that journey that gives us the pluck to write this book.

In reality, they are the true authors here. They once were lost. But now they have been drawn into Jesus—and they have something to teach us all about coming to faith.

THE POSTMODERN PATH TO FAITH

I can remember that afternoon as if it were yesterday. I (Doug) was standing out in the middle of the green grass of the quad on campus, singing as loudly as I could. Twenty of my Christian friends and I were holding guitars and singing to "witness" to the students who lounged nearby on the sunny patches of grass in the middle of the Cal Berkeley campus. We wanted to show our fellow students our authentic joy and love for Jesus. What better way to witness than with bold worship?

And man, did we grow that day! It was a profound faith experience for all of us who were willing to be "fools for Christ." We stood publicly and shamelessly for the gospel. Our faith was tested and affirmed.

But as for those who were trying to catch some rays on the lawn— well, no one was curious about issues of faith after our public spectacle. Instead of being attractive or intriguing witnesses for Christ, we were just one more random thing in their day, it seemed.

Our bold worship had grown our faith, but it made for weak evangelism. Our fatal flaw? We came up with our evangelistic strategy while we were alone in a room together with a bunch of Christians. Not once in our brainstorming and planning did we ask where our non-Christian fellow students were coming from. Not once did we try to find out what they might need to take a step toward Jesus. We were mostly coming up with something we wanted to do, not something that would be actually helpful to those unsuspecting sunbathers in the quad. I'll never forget that afternoon.

Over the past twenty years, we have had many such awkward moments as we slowly learned, helter-skelter, to walk the path of faith with our skeptical and cynical friends. Since that worship-on-the-grass event, God has granted us the humbling privilege of walking the journey of faith with more than two thousand people who were once lost but now are followers of Jesus.

Seeing all these conversions is exhilarating and humbling, because we clearly remember all the inglorious (and even embarrassing) moments that were part of the learning journey. But seeing all these folks coming to faith in Jesus has done something else to us as well: it has taught us about conversion.

Somewhere along the line we started asking the questions we never asked before going on the quad that afternoon: What is it like for those who are lost to take steps toward Jesus? And how can we truly be helpful to them on that journey?

There are two foundational truths about conversion that all these new believers have taught us over the years, two foundational truths about what it's like to become a Christian in this postmodern age.

IT'S MYSTERIOUS

The first lesson they have taught us about the path to faith is that it is, in the end, mysterious.

Again and again we found ourselves marveling at transformations that we never would have anticipated and shaking our heads in frustration at those who seemed near to faith but never got there. The gospel seeds that had been planted in some grew in spite of the weakness of our efforts. Other seeds that we tended with great care never took root.

Ultimately, the postmodern path to faith is a mystery. It reminds us of the truth of Jesus' parable in Mark 4:26-27: "This is what the kingdom of God is like. A man scatters seed on the ground. Night and day, whether he sleeps or gets up, the seed sprouts and grows, though he does not know how."

As kingdom farmers in postmodern soil, we must welcome this mysterious nature of that path to faith. In fact, there is something spiritually liberating when we admit and declare what is beyond us and where we are powerless. We cannot create life. It is impossible for us to predict why some of our friends will choose Jesus and why others just won't. We don't know how to change hearts. We don't know which seed will take root and which will bounce off the hardened ground.

This lesson has freed us from the modern temptation to view conversion as mostly a psychological phenomenon, an inner event that can be controlled and manipulated and triggered if we preach the gospel just right, sing the worship songs loud enough and dim the lights at just the right time. If conversion were psychological and controllable by humans, we'd be under a lot of pressure to get it done!

Our friends have reminded us that conversion is much more soul-deep and mysterious than all that. The path to faith is mysterious. To admit that is liberation. The monkey is off our back, and onto God's back, where it belongs. The Scriptures teach us that God is ultimately in control of salvation. No one, Jesus reminded his followers, can come all the way down the path to Jesus unless God calls them (John 6:44, 65).

When we plan outreach events, when we pray for our neighbors, when we consider whether to honestly answer the friend who asks about why we serve the poor, let us learn from the farmer in the parable. Let us look the seed in the eye and say, "You are a mystery to me. I am about to throw you out there, but I still don't know how you really work."

This is the first thing we have to learn from our new brothers and sisters about the postmodern path to faith in Jesus. And it is an important lesson to learn. It's important to hold on to this truth, because it is so tempting to grasp for control. Instead of living in this freeing biblical truth, we are often tempted to try to predict and reduce and control the mystery.

In order to keep embracing the truth of the mystery of conversion, we need to beware of declarations of certainty: This is how to program evangelism . . . This is how to share the gospel . . . This is how to reach seekers today . . . The postmodern new believers we've walked alongside would warn us against such declarations.

Heeding this lesson, we choose to humbly embrace the mystery of conversion like the farmer in the parable.

IT'S ORGANIC

The second lesson this group of new believers has shown us is that the postmodern path to faith is organic.

As we sat and listened to their stories we were struck immediately by the mystery but also by the similar seasons of growth that each of them went through.

Five distinct seasons, in fact. These were what we came to call "the five thresholds." While this second lesson surprised us, we have found it to be an equally important lesson to learn.

Remember how Jesus' parable ends? "All by itself the soil produces grain—first the stalk, then the head, then the full kernel in the head. As soon as the grain is ripe, he puts the sickle to it, because the harvest has come" (Mark 4:28-29). Heeding this lesson, we are able to recognize the different stages of growth (seed, stalk, head, full grain, ripe) and seek to love our non-Christian friends wisely and sensitively, adjusting to where they are in their growth.

The farmer in the parable can see the different stages of growth and act accordingly. Seeing this organic nature of heading to Jesus has freed us from the temptation to see conversion as primarily binary.

If our most sophisticated understanding of the path to faith says that our neighbor is either a Christian ("on") or not a Christian ("off"), then we tend to have just as unsophisticated a response to them. If they aren't a Christian, well, it's time to pull out our evangelism shotgun to try to force the switch to the "on" position. That's what it means to "do evangelism," after all. (Which tends to explain why we so rarely engage in evangelism.)

But just as no farmer would spend all her time scattering seeds, or all his time swinging a sickle, we see such one-trick evangelism as foolish spiritual farming. There are five distinct seasons of growth that we've noticed again and again. Realizing this organic way that people make their way down the path to faith frees us to respond to our friends' particular needs at the time.

While one-trick evangelists always seemed to annoy our friends, they've also told us that they never would have traveled all the way to Jesus if someone hadn't come along and helped them with the different parts of the journey they were on.

But if the path to faith really is organic, if there really are five distinct thresholds along the way to faith in Jesus, then is it really mysterious? Is conversion mysterious or organic?

IT'S BOTH

In the end, the path to Jesus is both mysterious *and* organic. Back to Jesus' whole parable:

> This is what the kingdom of God is like. A man scatters seed on the ground. Night and day, whether he sleeps or gets up, the seed sprouts and grows, though he does not know how. All by itself the soil produces grain—first the stalk, then the head, then the full kernel in the head. As soon as the grain is ripe, he puts the sickle to it, because the harvest has come. (Mark 4:26-29)

This image Jesus paints is full of tension, isn't it? At the same time it underlines the mysterious uncontrollable nature of conversion (the farmer sleeps and yet the seed grows in ways he can't understand) *and* the need for work (scattering seeds, harvesting with the sickle).

While it affirms the hidden nature of change (it happens at night when no one is looking), it also shows the natural, organic process that change follows (first seed, then stalk, then head, then the crop is ready).

While the growth of the plant is mysterious, it still follows nature. It is organic, and that means that for the seed to become a ripe plant, it will grow in a certain way.

This was the lesson our friends were teaching us. Each individual path to faith was a unique mystery. And their collective paths to faith had surprising similarities. These tremendous people who once were so jaded about Christianity and who are now dedicated believers have told us, in surprising unison, that the path to faith these days is both mysterious and organic. So their stories place us in a tension.

How do we stand in awe of the mysterious growth while at the same time helping them to the next natural threshold along the path? Well, living in that tension is what the five thresholds is all about.

THE FIVE THRESHOLDS OF POSTMODERN CONVERSION

So what are these similar landscapes along the path to faith, these so-called thresholds of postmodern conversion? Of course these look different in different people, they are paced differently, they are always experienced in the very real-life colors and contexts of each person. (Enough qualifiers yet?) But there *are* five significant shifts that tend to go on in postmodern folks as they come to faith.

First, our friends moved *from distrust to trust*. Somewhere along the line, they learned to trust a Christian. Mark was guarded and aloof. He did not trust us Christians. This kept him far away from exploring Jesus with us. It was impossible for him to shed that distrust. But then something wonderful and mysterious happened, and Mark crossed this threshold.

Second, they moved *from complacent to curious*. The fact that our friends actually came to trust a Christian didn't necessarily mean that they were at all curious about Jesus. Matthew, for example, had started trusting a Christian but was pretty uninterested in Jesus. Matthew was successful and had everything going for him and had no reason at all to be curious about Jesus. But then something wonderful and mysterious happened, and Matthew crossed this threshold.

Third, our friends moved *from being closed to change to being open to change in their life.* Interestingly, this always seemed to be the hardest threshold to cross—not for all of them but for most of them. Abner, for example, had started trusting some Christians and was even asking questions about Jesus. He was very curious. But he had no interest at all in examining his personal life. That was off limits. But then something wonderful and mysterious happened, and Abner crossed this threshold.

The fourth threshold is the move *from meandering to seeking.* Even when our friends became curious about Jesus and open to change in their life, it didn't necessarily follow that they began actively, purposefully seeking God. It was more natural for them to meander. Steve, for example, was very intrigued after some Christian students (whom he met sleeping in cardboard boxes at an event to raise awareness and dollars for the homeless) talked with him about Jesus. Steve accepted invitations to Bible studies, worship and even to a mission trip to Mexico. But he wasn't necessarily wanting to come to conclusions, to really seek answers. But then something wonderful and mysterious happened, and Steve crossed this threshold.

Finally, each of our friends had one more threshold to cross. They needed to *cross the threshold of the kingdom itself.* They needed to repent and believe and give their life to Jesus. Many people who journey well along the path to faith, learning to trust a Christian, becoming curious about Jesus, becoming open to personal change, even seeking after answers, never become Christians. Sarah might have been one of those folks. She was interested in Jesus, loved her new Christian friend and even went to conferences and Bible studies. But she was a scientist and couldn't imagine becoming a person of faith—not without physical proof. But then something wonderful and mysterious happened, and Sarah crossed the threshold into the kingdom itself.

WHAT DO YOU DO WITH THESE THRESHOLDS?

These foundational lessons about conversion have been freeing for us to learn. Understanding the mysterious nature of the path has freed us from activism and ushered us into a humble place of wonder and prayer. And understanding the organic nature of the path has freed us from the frustrations of one-trick evangelism and empowered us to get involved in the specific unfolding mysteries of our friends.

We can now look at someone and ask, "Where on the path are they?" Once we figure out more or less where they are, we can more easily empathize with their situation. We can fully appreciate the wonder and importance of where they are.

A few years ago, my (Doug's) son Mark Lee entered the first grade and ran up against a powerful threshold: reading. Though he was fluent with the alphabet, he could not put words together. He would look at the first letter of a word and then just throw out a wild guess. He was frustrated. Would he ever learn to read? It seemed impossible. For my part, I couldn't remember what it's like *not* to be able to read. Words instantly have meaning, and understanding seems to come naturally. Yet it would have been ridiculous for me to say, "What's the problem? Just read!"

We see learning to read as crossing over a threshold. On Mark Lee's side, the threshold seems intimidating and insurmountable. He almost can't imagine life on the other side. For us the threshold seems easy to cross, almost insignificant.

The spiritual thresholds that our non-Christian friends go through today are just like this. From where they stand, that next threshold seems insurmountable, no matter how obvious or easy it appears to us. They are in the land of the lost, which colors how each successive threshold appears to them.

Lostness, of course, looks different depending upon your perspective and personality. It is like getting lost while driving. Take our friend Jenny, for example. When she drives and gets lost, she is often so caught up in the scenery or the conversation that for a long time she doesn't even realize she is lost. She just keeps going farther and farther from her intended destination.

Then there are those like me (Doug). I know when I am lost, but I'm pretty sure I can figure it out by intuition. I admit I am lost, but I expect I'll find my way any minute now, as soon as I turn the next corner.

Finally, there are those smart people who know they are lost and know they need to get some directions. They stop and ask for help.

It's important to remember these different ways lostness can feel. "Lost" may be an accurate description of non-Christian friends from our perspective, but it may not feel like lostness to them. We can't know what each threshold feels like for the person going through it. But we can ask, and listen. This is what we did. We asked our friends to describe each threshold to us from their perspective. And here we try to use their words to talk about each part of the journey.

And the great news is the better we listen, the better we can serve those on the journey. If someone hasn't even crossed the first threshold, for example, we can stop handing them copies of *More Than a Carpenter* and realize they are at a place where considering the claims of Jesus isn't the issue; just trusting a Christian is the issue. And handing them that book (even if it's done out of love) might actually push them even further from crossing that first threshold.

Knowing where someone is on this postmodern path of faith can help us empathize with them. It can soothe our frustration as we realizc how insurmountable that next step may appear to them. And it allows us to ask another wonderful question: "How can I enter into the mystery of this stage of their growth?"

If a friend hasn't even begun trusting a Christian, we can stop hounding them to go to church with us and try to figure out how to build trust with them. If our neighbor has been past the first four thresholds for years and is an active seeker, we can stop trying to build trust and try to figure out how to help them cross the final threshold.

Of course, these thresholds are not magical or prescriptive. The reality is not everyone will cross a threshold, not everyone will become a Christian. Even if we become aware that someone hasn't even crossed the first threshold, that doesn't mean they will end up trusting us or any Christian—no matter how much we try to be trustworthy. Some people will never receive the seed. Jesus was very clear about this (for example, in Mark 4:14-19).

What these thresholds are is helpful. The more we heed the lessons of those who have walked this postmodern path to faith, the more freedom and joy we experience, and the better we are able to love our other postmodern friends.

In the next five chapters of this book we will look more carefully at each successive threshold. We will highlight their characteristics by telling the stories of some of our friends and will then consider what we have learned about stepping into the mystery of crossing each specific threshold with our friends. After walking through each of the five thresholds we will unpack the journey of new believers, followed by a few concluding thoughts on how to use the five thresholds.

If anything helpful comes of this, credit is due to our wonderful new brothers and sisters for their honesty and vulnerability and faith. Anything confusing or muddy likely comes from the two of us. We pray we might be faithful storytellers of those who once were lost but now are found.

TRUSTING A CHRISTIAN

"I wasn't the least bit interested in anything that came out of your mouth."

It was impossible for me (Doug) to become Mark's friend. He always avoided eye contact with me though I would smile and say hi as I passed him in the dorm. I had no idea what was going on in his heart and mind.

I was a senior and Mark was a freshman at Occidental College. He lived down the hall from me. But our paths were miles apart, because the guys on the water polo team had warned him, "Watch out for that Doug guy. He is the head of the 'God Squad' in the dorm."

Sometimes God builds trust between people in the most unexpected way. I knew that guys like to bond over sports. So on Friday afternoons we would roll out these old wrestling mats I had discovered, and about twenty of us would take turns wrestling each other behind the dorm.

Since I was a varsity wrestler in high school, I had a distinct advantage over a bunch of guys who were giving wrestling a shot for the first time. Mark was one of these guys.

Though Mark was willing to wrestle with me, he would never have entered into a spiritual conversation with me. He distrusted me and he was not looking for religion.

Mark got on the mat and we bonded over sweat. And then a small miracle happened within him. He decided that I was just like him. I was sweaty, fun, normal. I was no longer someone to be feared; I could be a friend.

After that he began to hang out in my room. I would leave my door open, hoping people would stop by and chat. When Mark came by, I put my book down, and Mark slowly told me his story.

Only later did I find out what exactly had happened on the wrestling mat. I could not see the revolution that was erupting within him. While he lived on the far side of the great divide of distrust, I looked liked an ogre. Once he passed through the threshold of trust, I looked like someone he could talk to, share life with and befriend.

AN ERA OF DISTRUST

Trust is sweet. It is better than gold. Trust is always a gift of the heart, and therefore it just may be the most precious thing in life, next to love. Trust between two people is so valuable and precious that it should never be taken for granted.

Once a friend told me (Doug) that she was giving me a special birthday present. On my birthday, she gave me a card that read, "I give you my trust." Holding that card in my hand, I understood the weight and beauty of what was being offered. I was deeply grateful.

What most of our friends have told us is that the process of coming to faith really gained traction for them once they started to significantly trust a Christian. There is an invisible wall between distrust and trust—a threshold. It seems that people must move through this threshold into trust in order for them to continue on to Jesus.

But why is this our starting place? Shouldn't we be talking about new ways of laying out the gospel? What about quoting verses for people? Can't we just focus on Bible verses that better connect with the postmodern generation? No, we can't. Relationships, genuine friendships are our currency.

Christa doesn't trust Christians because she was once told she's going straight to hell. A professor told Ryan that the Bible is full of mistakes. Bonnie read *The Da Vinci Code* and thinks the church is one big conspiracy. Julie was invited to a church outing but felt like an outsider the entire time.

In another day and age, God, religion and church enjoyed the general respect of the culture. Not today. Religion is suspect, church is weird, and Christians are hypocrites. Distrust has become the norm. People are tired of the "sales tactics" often employed by Christians and are offended by our bait-and-switch attempts at introducing them to Jesus. In the past, the occupation of evangelist was viewed as a respectable profession, even by secular society. Today evangelist has fallen to the very bottom of the pit, among the most distrusted occupations.

When people first find out we are Christians, we often literally see them shift from relaxed to rigid, from warm to suspicious. This is because when our friends first hear us call ourselves "Christian," several negative things often immediately flash through their minds: "Christians are self-righteous, and they always think they're better than me." "I'm about to get judged, so I better get my defenses up." "Christians are naive and narrow-minded, and they believe in fairy tales." "Christians are always pressing politics, so watch out!"

Don: On a recent airplane flight I got into a quite pleasant conversation with the person sitting next to me. He was a businessman from India. Even though I am quite introverted, I always love good, intelligent conversation—and this man was a great conversationalist. We spoke of some current events, ventured into politics, spoke of the regions and cultures we were from—and then he did it. He asked me what I did for a living. And I cringed.

I cringed because I am a campus pastor. And while I know that it is a blessing to have such spiritual matters brought up in the conversation, and while I am not in the least embarrassed about what I do, I knew that once he found out, that invisible but real shift would happen in our conversation. Sure enough, it did.

When he found out I was a Christian, he looked quite surprised. (I assumed he was surprised that he had actually been having an enjoyable conversation with a Christian.) Then he politely turned back to his magazine and kept his nose in it the rest of the flight.

I tried not to be frustrated. I knew that when it came to Christians this man was like many others—he was starting off with distrust. I wasn't starting on level ground in our conversation, I was starting in a hole.

When trust has not yet been established, lostness feels like wise skepticism and right thinking. If Christians are fanatical and narrow-minded, keeping one's distance seems like the smartest posture to take toward us. "There is something twisted about those smarmy Christians. And they want to fix me with that twisted agenda." Until this framework of distrust is shifted, growth is nearly impossible.

The good news is that we are not the first generation to face a context whose default is distrust. The apostle Paul faced an inherently skeptical audience as he traveled from city to city in the Roman Empire. Those who espoused a Hellenistic worldview were not impressed with his declaration of the resurrection. They did not begin with a posture of respect. In fact they looked down on this poser, mocking him as a "babbler" (Acts 17:18).

Paul was not offended or intimidated by their insults. Instead he found a way to press on and declare the good news. Let us learn like Paul to not only survive but thrive in our current context of distrust. Let us learn to be like Jesus, who "though he was in the form of God, did not count equality with God a thing to be grasped, but made himself nothing, taking the form of a servant, being born in the likeness of men" (Philippians 2:6 ESV).

God decided to incarnate himself, to come right alongside people. The Word didn't have to become flesh and "pitch a tent" right in our neighborhood. But he did (John 1:14). This is the incarnational way of God, his chosen way to bring people to himself. And it points the way for us, his children, to get along in this world as well. We aren't to preach at people from on high but to come alongside, to shake hands and befriend. To build trust.

And, as it turns out, this is exactly what people need these days to begin their journey to faith. In fact, the irony is that the more we listen to Scripture and history, the more we see the five thresholds as not merely for our current generation.

OUR FIVE KNEE-JERK REACTIONS TO DISTRUST

When the frigid air of distrust blows over us through a glance or comment, it is normal to react. Distrust hurts. It is unpleasant. After all, who wants to be rejected? If we are honest with ourselves, each of us has to admit that we are not eager to interact with people who are suspicious of us.

Often we react in ways that are less than loving, and sometimes we end up doing more to destroy trust than we do to build it. Awareness of these common destructive reactions within ourselves can help us identify our own temptations and keep us from just reacting blindly when someone starts off distrusting us. Here are five of the most common knee-jerk reactions to distrust that we have observed—and experienced.

1. Defend. Often when someone assumes negative things about us, we get defensive. *What's your problem? I am perfectly cool.* We know (or assume) there's nothing we personally have done wrong, and so we want to defend our reputation. *Hey, I'm not one of those televangelist types!* Sometimes we even want to defend whatever it is about Christianity that has caused distrust in them. *Look, if you really understood the Crusades . . .* While these defensive instincts are natural and instinctive, they are a pretty sure sign that we are starting to close our heart to the person who mistrusts us.

2. Bruise. Sometimes when we are not trusted, we feel personally offended. We become indignant. *Why would you not trust me? I can't believe I'm being treated this way, lumped stereotypically, unfairly, with other Christians.* We get offended that the other person feels offended, and no one really takes time to listen. Our ego is so bruised that we become reluctant to put our heart on the line again. Frequently, even though we wouldn't admit it, we allow disdain to grow in our heart. We see ourselves as the one who is persecuted, as the victim in the situation. (Don: On that airplane flight I must admit I felt a bit "persecuted," feeling as if I was being wrongly maligned.)

3. Avoid. Often our knee-jerk reaction to the neighbor who gets stiff and weird when they find out we are a Christian is to just avoid that neighbor ever after. We distance ourselves. *If they don't like me, then why bother? Who wants to wade through their baggage with past Christians?* It's easier to just avoid the awkwardness and gravitate toward those who "get me"—other Christians. We become numb and indifferent. We stop caring.

4. Judge. Out of feelings of hurt, and out of pride, some of us lash back with a condescending attitude. It seems so ridiculous that our non-Christian friends would look down on us that we point the finger right back. (Or at least want to.) *I can't believe this immoral, pot-smoking New Ager is actually looking down their nose at me!* Whenever we feel under the gun, it's natural to want to turn the situation and point the gun at someone else.

5. Argue. Some of us are good at debating, and when others react to the fact that we are "one of those Christians," we receive their distrust as a challenge. We rev up to unleash some potent logic on them. *Look out for my apologetics. Hear this and weep!* We get into a competitive mindset and don't want to lose the point. As we argue, we can deceive ourselves into thinking we are actually serving them, helping them along toward Jesus, but often this reactionary posture actually works to derail their journey of faith. Sure, arguing is a natural reaction; it's just not always a *helpful* reaction.

Don: When I am honest with myself I have to admit that my most common reaction to people who have issues with Christians is just to avoid them. Maybe I just don't sit near them. Or maybe I sit by them but do everything I can to make sure the fact that I am "one of those Christians" doesn't come up.

When I got a job at a county recreational facility back in Tacoma, Washington, one summer, I joined a crew of wonderfully interesting, dynamic men who were pretty jaded about most things. I even heard a couple of disparaging remarks about Christians early on that summer.

How did I respond to this "hostile" environment? I did everything I could to avoid getting their jadedness and mistrust pointed my way. I steered clear of certain topics and even (I am being honest here) answered a few questions of theirs a little less than accurately! I didn't purposefully do any of this. It's not as if I developed a strategy of avoidance as I entered the situation. Rather, this was how I naturally reacted to their distrust. It was a sort of knee-jerk response of my heart.

Knowing this about myself is clarifying. And helpful. It helps me pray for help. It helps me notice sooner in the process that I am actually avoiding. My guess is we all deal with avoidance at some level and could all use a call to courage and a reminder that Jesus promised us (it was a *promise*) that we would not be treated well by everyone.

Knowing this about my heart also helps me know which kingdom habits I need to purposefully practice in order to build trust.

FIVE KINGDOM HABITS TO BUILD TRUST

In any friendship, trust develops over time. It could take anywhere from one day to years, depending on how much distrust the non-Christian is carrying or whether they have any at all. And trust in any friendship is a dynamic thing. There's no guarantee that once we have crossed the "trust line" with a non-Christian they will magically trust us forever.

There is, however, a basic threshold of trust that they will need to cross before evangelism can effectively happen. Though some people are naturally much better than others at building trust, we can all practice the five trust-building habits in this chapter—and the bond will grow.

We need to learn to be unfazed by distrust. We are in an age of distrust, so instead of being surprised and reactionary when our coworkers or neighbors don't trust us, we need to learn how to respond kindly and quickly begin the normal, basic and foundational investment of trust-building.

These kingdom postures of building trust aren't just a necessity in times of great distrust: they are always the kingdom call. This is the call of love. It is the way of Jesus. Jesus leaned in toward people, asked them to "come and see" his life, went to their weddings and parties. He took on flesh and pitched a tent among people. He incarnated.

One of the more obvious results of this was that people were comfortable with him, were drawn to him—especially (and this is an important point) those who were lost, far away from God. Those who tried to keep their distance from such needy, dirty lost people were furious at Jesus for this. Eating with all the wrong people he was. But as the author of Hebrews points out, the fact that Jesus was "made like his brothers and sisters in every way" means he is able to sympathize with our weaknesses; folks feel free to draw near to him with confidence (Hebrews 2:17; 4:14-16). And that's just what people did. They came to Jesus; they came close to him with confidence.

Jesus wasn't content to presume upon whatever modicum of honor rabbis naturally received; he was always trying to build trust, to make connections, intimate connections, between himself and those he met on the road. He could have healed lepers from a distance, but instead he touched them. He could have been fed by angels, but instead he accepted invitations into the kitchens of those he met along his way.

While this is always the call for us, it is an especially wise and blessed route to take in the type of distrustful age we're swimming in these days. Here are a few simple, practical ways we can purposefully build trust rather than give in to our knee-jerk reactions to distrust.

1. *Pray.* When we feel the temptation to defend, we can instead choose to stop and pray. As we catch ourselves getting defensive, we can silently ask God to soften our heart. We can admit that we are hurt or irritated by the other's distrust. We can be honest with God about our struggles. By bringing our defensiveness to God, we are letting him do a deeper work in us. "Jesus, you love this person enough to give your life for them. Please infuse my heart with your love and passion for them. Help me see them the way you see them."

We can also pray for *them*, intercede for the stuff in their life—their family, their concerns, their hopes and joys and struggles. There's nothing like going onto our knees for someone to help open our hearts to them. As we take the time to try to think up a petition or two to utter on their behalf, something mysterious and wonderful may happen to us. As we consider their life, as we contemplate their fears and concerns so that we might intercede for them, as we wrap their life and specific circumstances and relationships in prayer, our own heart begins to soften toward them. We find it somehow easier to embrace them—or at least care a little about them.

As we are on our knees in prayer, God somehow shares his own parental affection for them with us. And this makes it much easier to lose the tight defensive posture we first had and goes a long way toward enabling trust. When you feel the urge to defend, pray.

2. *Learn.* When we feel the temptation to bruise and feel offended, we should choose to learn. We can try to understand the world from the other person's perspective and sympathize with them. Instead of being victimized by their distrust, we can try to *learn about* their distrust—where it comes from, what has happened to them. Instead of being offended, we can choose to enjoy and accept them. We can even allow God to captivate us with them.

In Mark 5, as Jesus is on his way to the house of Jairus (an important official) we see Jesus stop as he encounters a hurting, bleeding woman. Jesus doesn't just brush her off; he doesn't heal her wounds quickly so he can keep moving. He leans forward toward her, with all his attention and care focused on her. To the shock of those in the crowd (and perhaps to our shock as well), Jesus makes time to let this woman who had bled for twelve years tell her "whole story," detail by detail. How long did that take? Long

The Trust Inventory: How Much Trust Do You Have?

To help you think through how much trust you currently have with a friend or family member, ask yourself some simple questions about that relationship:

- Have they ever called me when they had a problem?
- Have I ever called them for help in anything?
- Have they ever been real with me when they were angry or sad?
- Do I hide my honest emotions or moods from them?
- Have they ever asked me for advice?
- Do we ever just have fun together?
- When do I feel most connected with them—and what are we doing then?

enough for Jairus's daughter to die. Jesus listens to the woman, and he listens well. Jesus knows how to be present with people. After hearing her story, he knows that she needs physical healing *and* social healing. So before the entire crowd, he pronounces her clean and affirms her faith, easing her journey back into mainstream society. He has taken the time to listen for the deeper need.

Following Jesus' lead and being a learner means that we too ask good questions, even of those who are annoying or distrustful. Jesus lets people capture his whole attention. He is captivated by them, their story, their yearnings, their needs. He listens to their "whole story" and shows us how to be intrigued with each person's uniqueness. No two people have the same upbringing, the same hopes and dreams, the same fears. Instead of cringing and feeling bruised by their distrust, we must lean into them and learn.

Don: When my wife and I first moved into our condo, I met one of our near neighbors, Rose. Rose was a retired schoolteacher. My first impression was that she was a somewhat grouchy woman and set in her ways. She came over to let me know that I had used the recycling bin incorrectly! She always had a furrowed, thoughtful brow. In another of our early conversations (I think as she asked me what I did for a living), it became silently clear to me that not only was Rose not a Christian but there was a mound of distrust inside her toward us. A couple of barbed comments, and I felt mightily misunderstood and oppressed.

Now at this point my temptation was to sigh deeply, play the victim and avoid Rose as much as possible. Why subject myself to her sharp (though quite witty) barbs? But I resisted these knee-jerk reactions and instead chose to learn more about Rose. I asked her a few questions and found that she was quite interesting. A friendship started to form. Eventually we spoke in detail about God and Jesus and religion and her thoughts and feelings and experiences. We shared meals. We watched TV together. We played poker.

Now, three years later, Rose is one of our best friends. We enjoy her and hang out with her and—we really love her. I can't imagine my life without her. Slow conversations with her are one of the highlights of my week. If I had sat bruised as a victim, her distrust for Christians would have only grown. But now she has crossed threshold one—she trusts a Christian. And my life is all the richer for that. I understand more all the time why Jesus was just so captivated by people. The habit of being a learner has strengthened my heart, enriched my life and communicated love to Rose.

People can smell a fake from a mile away. The rest of this book will be totally useless if you don't practice giving your heart away, going deeper in relationships with non-Christians. We can never treat people like projects. Give your heart. People need to know that you accept them and like them. When you are feeling bruised, choose to lean in and learn.

3. Bond. When we feel the temptation to avoid, we can choose to bond instead. Rather than walking wide circles around someone, we can walk right up and do what they do with them.

Jesus pitched a tent in our neighborhood. He displaced himself, humbly, for us. This becomes our model. He loved us enough to get onto our turf. In leaving his comfort zone in heaven, he displaced himself and chose to walk with us through life. In the end, Jesus was accused of being a drunkard. It's one thing to "accept" people as they are; it's another to actually go to a party to be with them. Jesus chose to be with people. In calling the first disciples, he didn't send out letters from the synagogue and ask them to meet him there. He cruised the docks. He walked along the shore. He got into their boats. He went fishing.

We too can get involved in the lives of those around us. Instead of taking an instinctive step backward, we can take purposeful kingdom steps forward.

When our neighbors have a Super Bowl party or barbecue, do we go? What about Little League, the theater, or other hobbies such as sailing, scrapbooking, book clubs and gardening? The possibilities are endless. Everyone could use a buddy at Home Depot. In our place of work, do we see lunch outings and happy hours as opportunities to be with people, or do we pooh-pooh the seemingly trivial, secular conversation? We've found that our most fruitful conversations with people happen while driving somewhere in the car together, sitting next to each other at the baseball game, digging in each other's gardens, walking our kids together to the park, wrestling in a dorm, waiting for a movie to start. The best conversations with non-Christians rarely occur inside a church building or at an event designed for seekers, and you don't have to be a student living in a dorm to find ways of bonding with those non-Christians God has placed in your life.

Don: Years ago I lived next door to a few men. These guys were real partiers, and since our apartments were next door to each other, they often invited me to party with them. I never went. We had a cordial relationship (they raided our fridge when they had the munchies, we borrowed their amazing gas barbecue grill) but nothing more. One day Nick, one of the guys, told me he was heading out to nearby Eldora Canyon and asked if I would want to come along. I had plenty to do that day but decided to tag along. And as we hiked up into the mountains (it was one of his favorite trails) we naturally started talking about the deepest things of life. This was where he felt most comfortable; this was where he got reflective. Because I went to where he was, the trust between us grew tremendously.

The best tool to keep ourselves from avoiding non-Christians is to spend time with them. Not everyone will want to bond with us, of course. But if we want to help our friends cross threshold one, it is incumbent upon us to open our schedule and make them a priority in our busy life—to be willing to be displaced ourselves for the sake of building trust. Prayer is not actually enough. Even genuine prayer. We have to hang out with folks in person. We combat avoidance with bonding.

4. Affirm. When we feel the temptation to judge, we can instead choose to affirm. We're not talking about a blind, indiscriminate affirmation of everything, though. Even kids can see through that cheap, meaningless golf-clap affirmation. We're talking about looking for real good and affirming it.

In Acts 17, addressing Athenians who are entangled in extreme idol worship, Paul speaks in an interesting way. It would be understandable, even expected, for him to utterly blast these heathens for their egregious violation of the Second Commandment. You can almost see it coming. In fact many of us would have done just that. Our offense at their immoral behavior would have trumped any loving desire to help them come closer to Jesus. We are so quick to pull out our morality

Three Pitfalls to Avoid

1. **Avoid relativism.** *As you seek to build trust through affirmation, learning and going into someone else's world, you need to be careful to be honest about the uniqueness of Christ. You will actually be doing your friends a disservice if, in the name of trying to build trust, you pretend that all religions are the same and can lead to God. No one likes a bait-and-switch. You need to be clear in your own mind what is unique about Jesus. It will be hard to walk with your friends into the Jesus revolution if you don't know yourself what is revolutionary about Jesus.*

2 **Be with them, but don't sin.** *You want to get on their turf as best you can, but you shouldn't participate in activities that compromise your character or integrity. It's not worth it to break the law or do what you know to be sin. Find other ways to get on their turf.*

3. **Don't walk unwisely into temptation.** *Know what your struggles are. If you know you struggle with alcoholism, it might not be a very good idea to follow your coworkers to the bar after work. This caution is similar to the second but is more about knowing your own limitations. Even if something isn't sin, it still might be harmful to your spirituality. Be thoughtful about your own temptations, and make wise decisions based on that self-knowledge.*

pistols and start firing away. Even when we resist the urge, our minds are often so focused on the sins of non-Christians we meet that we can see little else.

But to our surprise Paul *affirms* these folks. Yes, he affirms them. He works hard to find something good in this practice of theirs: "I see that in every way you are very religious" (v. 22). He affirms that they are seeking after God. He doesn't distance himself from their idolatry. He honors them for wanting to worship something. He sees his role as affirming kingdom impulses within them and then pointing them to Jesus. This is a powerfully disarming habit, forging bonds of real trust.

We struggle to emulate Paul in this. We fear affirming sin in our friends and so we say nothing, or we just judge. Maybe we turn a blind eye and naively tell them, "It's all good." We might be shocked if God showed us today how many of our non-Christian friends' values are worth affirming: the gay activist's commitment to equality, the Muslim coworker's sacrificial weekend involvement in caring for the poor. Unfortunately, these often go unnoticed. We don't look hard enough to see and affirm the spiritual impulses of our Buddhist neighbors or the real humility before nature of the stoned guy next door or the great parenting skills of the mom who dabbles in Wicca.

Where there is distrust, our aloofness can come across as judgment. We have the power to combat this by looking for good in people and affirming it. That habit builds trust.

5. *Welcome.* When we feel the temptation to argue against the family member who doesn't trust us because we are a Christian, we can choose instead to welcome them into our life. Instead of posturing ourselves over and against them, we can welcome them with open arms into our world. This habit is vulnerable and risky. It has a way of disarming our combative posture and reminds us of Jesus.

In John 1 Jesus offers some brand-new acquaintances the incredible gift of hospitality, "Come and see," he says. They are curious about him, and he invites them into his world. They get to come and see, to get to know him by seeing who he really is. Jesus wants to spend time with them instead of preaching a sermon to them. He's not pushy; he simply invites them in and opens up an opportunity for deeper relationship. "Come and see" is one of the most authentic, transparent gifts we can give. It is better than any pat answer we might offer.

When folks are curious and frustrated about the mystery of who Jesus is (Matthew 11:1-19), he similarly opens his arms of hospitality and transparency: "What do you think? What do you see in my life?" Jesus' life is an open book. He knows that his lifestyle and priorities will speak volumes.

In the early church we also see this revolutionary formation of a "come and see" Christian community (see, for example, Acts 2). These folks, like Jesus, opened their lives and hearts. They gave the grace of hospitality. Trust was built as their lives reflected a love and a power that went beyond human reason. They were a people of great hospitality and generosity and sacrificial service. And they invited people into this life of theirs.

We can never stop at going into people's worlds to build trust; we must also invite people into our own world. We can open our heart, our home, our lifestyle and our friendships to them. We offer a profound grace to folks as we ask them to "come and be with us."

Don: I think I did the smartest thing ever when I married my wife, Wendy. For many reasons. One of the reasons it's such a blessing to partner with Wendy is how unimaginably hospitable she is. Around Wendy people feel at home. She has our kitchen table regularly full of people. I never know who will be at the dinner table when I come home. And I always know I can invite anyone over for a meal. There will always be plenty of food, and Wendy will always be thrilled to have someone else at the table. Time and time again I've seen how this kind of table fellowship sows kingdom seeds and softens up the rocky ground of distrust.

When someone comes into my home to eat at our table, they can relate with Wendy and the kids, they can see what we do as a family, what our meals together are like, how we relate, how we talk with Christian friends who are also present. Our lives become an open book because of that table and what Wendy makes happen there. "Come and see" sounds more like "come and eat" at our place, but the principle is the same.

We combat the temptation to argue and push away through opening our arms in hospitality. Come and see, we say. And in this way distrust begins to melt and trust is built in unimaginable ways.

THE BEGINNING OF A JOURNEY

According to the testimonies of hundreds of folks who once were lost, their journey toward Jesus began when they trusted a Christian. Once we learn this truth, we are free to love those non-Christians in our lives who are at threshold one by helping them move from distrust to trust. We can become more self-aware about our knee-jerk temptations. And we can resolve to practice more helpful kingdom habits that make trust more possible.

When God's Spirit moves and uses our small acts of love to help someone across this threshold, it is the first step on what may just be a life-changing journey.

After Mark began to trust me (Doug) on the wrestling mat (crossing threshold one), curiosity quickly followed. His questions poured forth. We looked at Jesus together in the Scriptures, I told him about my experiences of God, and he hung around the community of friends with whom I followed Jesus. Seeing our lives and our love for each other, he was soon ready to seek God for himself. By January of that same academic year, he had entered the kingdom of God. He became a follower of Jesus. My heart exploded with joy! Within a few months, he and I were serving together once a week at an urban youth center, tutoring kids who needed help to get out of the cycle of gangs and drugs.

Helping our friends warm up to God is what makes life rich and meaningful. Mark and I stayed close friends after I graduated. He was a groomsman in my wedding. Then he spent a few years in Russia, walking the path of faith with other university students as I had walked with him a few years before.

Today Mark is using his gifts to influence millions of investment dollars around the globe for the sake of justice and righteousness. We keep in touch by Skype. He is one of my heroes. Seeing friends like Mark cross the threshold of trust means the world to me.

Becoming Curious

"I liked you and liked that you were different from most Christians, but I've just never been interested in religious stuff. Ever."

It was a warm spring day in Colorado when I (Don) first met Matthew. Matthew was a student at the University of Colorado, a music major who was extraordinarily gifted and who had plenty of baggage regarding Christians. Matthew had heard me give a talk at a Christian service on campus, and a friend of his introduced us afterward. Matthew wanted to get together and talk about some of his questions about Christians, so we started hanging out every couple weeks or so.

At first Matthew was pretty careful around me. He had so many frustrations with Christians, and since I too was a Christian I could sense his guardedness. We would get together, he would vent his honest frustrations about Christians, and for the most part I just agreed with him. I could have tried to defend our track record, but we Christians actually have done various insensitive and oppressive things over the years, so I didn't feel the need to defend right off the bat. My honest agreement surprised him, and over time he started warming up. We would meet at a coffee shop or a bar and just talk about his frustrations, and in this way, slowly over time, Matthew crossed threshold one—he trusted me.[1]

As we became friends, Matthew began asking me about my life. I talked honestly about what was going on. One day as I was telling him about my family's upcoming summer move into Sun Valley (statistically one of the poorest, most dangerous neighborhoods in Denver), Matthew stopped me. He just didn't get it. Why would I take my pregnant wife and one-year-old son to live in Sun Valley?

"Well, Jesus taught that . . . I realize this may sound kind of crazy, but Jesus taught that the poor on this earth are blessed spiritually. They are in on some stuff that the rich may never quite grasp. In fact, Jesus said they were—*lucky*."

Matthew stared at me. "Lucky? What are you talking about?"

Then we talked about how much time Jesus spent with the poor and how Jesus told his followers that when they care for the poor they are really caring for him. We talked about Mother Teresa and what she said about why she went to be with the poor. As we talked, Matthew's eyes grew thoughtful.

He had never known all this about Jesus. Having no interest in being with the poor himself, he was perplexed by my plans for the summer and how that was related to my following Jesus. Jesus' word was changing my life and revolutionizing my decisions—this was a parable to him that burned in his brain.

---

[1]Yes, I did say "bar." Let me explain. Scripture is very clear about drunkenness—it is a foolish thing. (And for someone who has previously struggled with addiction, even *being* in a bar can be foolish.) While I am very careful about what I drink, I have no problems going into a bar to have a conversation with someone. Matthew was very surprised when I first had a beer in front of him, and interacting in this everyday way was a part of what helped him cross the first threshold from distrust to trust.

Later in the same conversation I asked Matthew if he had ever read much about Jesus himself. I thought back and realized that all our conversations had centered on Christians: their history, their culture, their habits. But Matthew had never really discussed Jesus. Matthew thought about it. He shook his head slowly and said, "No, I guess I don't know that much about Jesus."

As this self-realization dawned, I told him about each of the Gospels and suggested he read the Gospel of Mark over the summer. That summer, even though Matthew was busy with an important internship over on the East Coast, he did read Mark. Then he went on to read all four of the Gospels. He found Jesus thrilling and couldn't read enough about him. Somewhere during our conversation Matthew had crossed the second threshold: he moved from complacency to curiosity. It was a beautiful shift.

CURIOSITY CHANGES LIVES

Just because someone trusts you it doesn't necessarily follow that they are super curious about Jesus. In fact, many non-Christians are content to have a Christian friend or two but never get any closer to the kingdom.

After coming to trust a Christian, they face a whole new threshold. The process of moving from complacent about Jesus to curious about him is the second major threshold our friends have told us they went through on their way to faith.

To go from being complacent about spiritual things to being intrigued is a natural process. Our souls and our minds are built by God to be curious, to ask questions until we have landed upon satisfying answers. So this move from complacent to curious isn't easy (complacency is easier, of course), but it taps into a desire and need that is wired into all people.

Before crossing this threshold, our lost friends may seen apathetic to us, but to them it might feel more like contentment. "It's all good." They don't want to make waves. They are just making life work, just getting by. And they are working at being tolerant: "Whatever is true for you is true for you, and whatever is true for me is true for me." This is what they have been taught since kindergarten. It is a bland view of the world, but it is a view they are very accustomed to. Jesus would like to awaken them to a Technicolor view of life, but this can be a slow journey.

Most folks don't go from being spiritually complacent to bursting with curiosity overnight. Curiosity tends to blossom over time. You can think of curiosity as having three levels of intensity: awareness, engagement and exchange.

First comes awareness. Matthew had never thought about what might be good about moving into an urban neighborhood. Such thoughts had never crossed his mind before. He suddenly became *aware* of options he had never considered. His personal experience was no longer enough to allow him to understand the world. This propelled him to take a step out of his take on the world and ask questions.

Awareness of more options, more paths in life, is often the first baby step out of complacency. As people hear about Jesus, their old answers and old pictures of God slowly become antiquated and inadequate. This awareness of a new and different reality is a first step.

Just being aware of something new doesn't necessarily mean you are really, really curious, though. *Engagement* is a more intense flavor of curiosity. Matthew began to engage when he asked to hang out with Don. He took this personal engagement a step further when he began reading the Gospels on his own. Engaging with a real Christian, becoming friends with a Christian and taking time to read through the life of Jesus were concrete actions that caused Matthew's curiosity to grow stronger over time.

But we all know it's quite possible to show up at an event but not really show up. Matthew engaged by reading the Gospels. But he also entered into *exchange*. This is an intense form of curiosity that means being so curious that you want to exchange ideas, ask questions and offer your own opinions. This expression of curiosity is more than just cognitive activity. Matthew wasn't just quietly listening to what Don had to say; he was right there in the mix sharing his own opinions about Christianity and asking all sorts of questions. This type of give-and-take was important because Matthew was not just a passive hearer. He was actively involved in the topic, and in this way his curiosity continued to develop and grow.[2]

Given how wonderful it is to see someone grow curious about Jesus, is it possible to help our friends move there from the complacent place they are in now? What we have found is that the Spirit often uses regular folks to help people get across this significant threshold.

---

[2]It's important to remember here that even when someone's curiosity grows very strong, this does not mean that they are open to actual change in their life (threshold three) or are truly seeking for answers and conclusions (threshold four). They are simply investigating and allowing themselves to hear new ideas. They are curious. Which is wonderful!

A common mistake, though, is for Christians to mistake someone's curiosity for either genuine openness or seeking. While moving from complacent to curious, people often investigate Jesus and his teachings, and they can ask quite provocative questions. For all intents and purposes, they appear quite interested. In their heart of hearts, however, they are not yet planning on making any real changes in their life. Curiosity should be celebrated as a step forward, not mistaken for something it's not.

PROVOKE CURIOSITY

Jesus was the king of provoking curiosity in those around him. It's striking to watch Jesus walk along the roads and towns of Israel and draw great interest and crowds wherever he went. Much of this attention can be credited to his miraculous healing powers, of course. But we also see Jesus, as he interacts with folks more intimately, doing simple things to intentionally stir them toward curiosity.

Jesus knew what the crowds expected of him, and he often did the opposite. They wanted him to stay, and he went on to other towns. They wanted him to bash Rome, and he suggested they pay taxes. Jesus asked questions, told parables and did the most unexpected things. We can emulate Jesus by engaging in these simple actions ourselves. Doing so, we have found, is a great service to our friends who are stuck (impossibly stuck, it would seem) at threshold two.

1. Encourage questions. Jesus often asked questions of those around him. This seems normal, but when you consider that Jesus knew everything already, it makes you rethink why Jesus did ask so many questions. It seems Jesus used questions not to elicit information from people but rather to stir within them some thought or emotion.

Jesus is asked 183 questions in the Gospels. He answers just 3 of them—and he asks 307 questions back! As our friend Tom says, "Jesus does not have Q and A sessions. He has Q and Q sessions."[3]

- "What do you want me to do for you?" (The guy's a paralytic desperately living life on the off-chance he'll be healed at the pool near him. Isn't it obvious to everyone what he wants?)

- "How do you read the law?" (This posed to an expert in the law who

---

[3]Thanks to Tom Hughes for counting all those questions. Impressive!

was mostly interested in taking shots at what Jesus had to say.)

- "Where is everyone? Has no one condemned you?" (This to a woman caught in adultery after everyone had humbly walked away rather than stone her.)

- "Who do people say I am?" (Though he must have already known this!)

- "What are you looking for?" (They were looking for him, but he wanted them to look again at their desires.)

A seminary professor we know says, "A good question is worth a thousand answers." Sometimes when someone asks us a question, an answer is the last thing they need. Instead, they need someone to stoke the fire of curiosity in their soul. They need someone to awaken intrigue within them by giving them another question rather than a pat answer.

One of the greatest acts of love we can give is to ask good questions and help our friends learn to ask more questions for themselves. We live in an age of too much information, too few good questions. Let's be the ones to ask the great questions. Spark curiosity wherever you go, just like Jesus. Let's be like Jesus: let's ask intriguing questions that help our friends think about life from angles they have never considered.

2. Use parables. Jesus often told simple yet haunting stories to those around him. These parables were stories or images that stuck inside the minds of the hearers like fishhooks. Once stuck into someone, these seemingly innocent stories haunted: they begged further inquiry, further thought, further questions.

In Mark 4 Jesus clarifies that what he loves most about parables is that they draw some people closer to him—they make people come closer

Ask Starter Questions to Encourage Questioning

Learning to ask good questions can be awkward. We think that becoming better conversationalists should just happen naturally. Many people are offended by the idea that they might need training on how to ask questions, and being handed a "good question" to use in conversations feels trite.

But we actually lead seminars on asking good questions. We are convinced that few skills are more pivotal for people who want to walk with their friends in the journey of faith. What questions do you tend to use as you help conversations move toward spiritual things? When training, I (Doug) suggest that everyone find a few comfortable questions that work for them.

Look at the questions below and find a few that work for you. Don't scorn these questions just because they look simple or obvious. Try them out with a Christian friend until you are comfortable guiding a conversation deeper.

- *Have you ever had a spiritual experience? Would you like to have one?*
- *Have you ever felt like you received a sign from God? What would you do if God gave you a sign?*
- *What is your take on this whole God question? What do you think God is like?*
- *Why do so many people hide behind religion? What do you think is wrong with Christians today?*
- *What do you think life is about? Do you think you have a destiny?*
- *Do you think that people are more spiritually interested today than they were five years ago?*
- *What is the most significant thing that has happened to you in the last month?*

You might be surprised how getting your mouth used to asking certain provocative questions will serve you later on when you're in a conversation. Getting better at asking questions is a way of serving our friends.

for clarification. Many yawned at his parables, but some were perplexed, wanting to ask more, probe more, know more. In fact, those who probed his simple little parables, wanting to peer into their depths, had, in the words of Jesus, discovered the "secret of the kingdom."

These parables are short and memorable. And we still talk about them today: The story of a dad and his two sons. The story of a desperate widow and a mean judge. The image of a pearl, a hidden treasure, seeds being thrown onto soil. Jesus used these seemingly everyday images and stories to draw people closer to him, to arouse curiosity in those around him. Ultimately they were genius teaching tools, of course, as he unpacked the deep, profound, earth-shattering messages they contained. But their initial purpose was to invite inquiry, curiosity.

Not only would it behoove us to learn and use the parables of Jesus and all they contain, but we also could do a better job of noticing the parables all around us today.

Jesus wasn't above using the everyday as a window to the spiritual. He used the sight of impressive temple walls and the recent news of a tower falling on some people to bring up spiritual realities in his conversations. Simple images and stories that can pull people into deeper questions are all around us today, too. We can find these modern-day parables in art, at the movies, in a sports arena, in the latest bestsellers, in the news, on our very own streets, and in the various hoses of technology that spray into our lives daily.

Instead of waiting every couple of years for an image or story that takes up Christian themes to dominate our cultural landscape (think *The Passion of the Christ, The Da Vinci Code,* etc.) and then working ourselves into an evangelical frenzy to capitalize on this oh-so-obvious chance to talk with non-Christians about Jesus, we should practice the regular habit of noticing parables all around us and learning how to use them to provoke curiosity about Jesus.

Mostly this just means paying closer attention to the world. While driving to work, you hear a story on NPR about how being a permanent detainee in a prison without any hope of release destroys people's psyches. *Hmm . . . without hope the human soul gets destroyed. Sounds familiar . . . perhaps I'll bring the report up in the lunchroom today and see where the conversation goes.* Pay attention; practice using parables. That'll go a long way in helping you provoke curiosity.

3. Live curiously. Jesus was surprising. It wasn't that he was going for cheap shocks; he just did things all the time that were countercultural and caused those around him to pause and stare. And ask questions.

The Pharisees were shocked and wanted to know why Jesus had touched the leper, why he was eating with sinners and tax collectors, why he was letting the prostitute cry all over his feet. The disciples wanted to know why Jesus kept provoking the authorities all the time, why he insisted on heading to Jerusalem when tensions were so high, why he allowed little kids to take up so much of his important time.

This shows us a bit of why pointing to Jesus is so crucial in helping people become curious (see our next point about focusing on Jesus) but also gives us an example of how we can provoke more curiosity with our own lives.

Matthew's curiosity got way dialed up when he saw that Don was going to go down to Sun Valley for the summer. This was a seemingly ridiculous, very surprising thing to do. Such kingdom-oriented, countercultural actions, when lived out in our daily lives, can help our friends cross this threshold into curiosity.

The same is true of our words. Jesus always had an unexpected word for those who came to him. The marginalized expected to be treated like second-class citizens, but Jesus honored them and made them the focus of the crowd. The arrogant expected to be applauded by Jesus, but he exposed their folly and invited them to become lowly. Everyone had a preconceived notion of which box Jesus fit in, and Jesus stirred their curiosity by refusing to fit their assumptions about him.

What do your coworkers think about you? What box do they have you in? How do they expect a "nice Christian" to say in various situations and conversations? Try saying unexpected and borderline outlandish things to stir curiosity.

In the end, even if you are encouraging questions, using parables and living curiously, it is important to remember that curiosity grows over time. Sometimes this threshold takes time. Hang in there with your friends. Often the soil can look barren and unworthy of the sweat and toil, but as we dig and help uncover their curiosity we will find rich patches of ground for seeds to take root and sprout new life. Often you will find that provoking curiosity in others makes your life more interesting than it's been in a while.

Doug: My friend Crystal came over to my apartment rather discouraged. She had been trying to love and bond with non-Christians on campus all year. She joined them in their hobbies and activities. She accepted them. She enjoyed them. She prayed for them. She served them. But she was stuck. Their concept of her was that she was kind. They found a "nice person" box and fit her nicely in it. But they were not curious about her life, her God or her faith. They felt no need to ask her questions because they had found a box to contain her. No curiosity.

Crystal and I talked about how Jesus is provocative. He is intriguing, outlandish at times, adamantly refusing to fit into anyone's box. They get out the box with his name on it, and he kicks it down with his unexpected answers. They bring out their best either-or question, and he paves a third way they never considered. They are left speechless. I suggested that Crystal answer questions with a question. And if her friends were not asking questions, she could ask her own out loud.

Sitting in people's dorm rooms, she began to ponder out loud, "I wonder how many people are interested in spiritual things on this campus. How many people are ready to change their lives for something better?" These questions burned in people's minds.

As an African American, she would add, "People of color are looking for God on this campus. People of color pray." To white non-Christians, this was provocative, unexpected. How should they respond to her? They just looked at her, soaked it up, eyes wide open. She was making them aware of things they had never considered.

She started inviting everyone in the dorm to go feed the homeless with her. She challenged them to open their closets and bring extra clothes to give away—opening up paths to them they had never considered.

Crystal was doing a beautiful thing in their postmodern world. She was a catalyst of curiosity, and God was working through her to disrupt people's easy answers about life. Seeds were being planted.

Practicing Christian community is also pivotal to living curiously. Like Crystal, there are some things you can do individually to intrigue. But there are many, many kingdom realities that are seen only through relationships and community. Let your friends watch you do life together with your small group, and they will see forgiveness in action, reconciliation, people who speak the truth in love to each other, honoring one another with their words, healthy cross-gender relationships, care for the poor, the power of prayer. As you practice generosity and care for those in need in your church, bring your non-Christian friends with you. God's generosity is seen in your generous acts.

In Acts 2, Christians share their possessions in common with each other. Inspired by this, I (Doug) began loaning my car out to friends who wanted to borrow it. My non-Christian friends were curious (and happy to get a car to drive). They asked questions because they saw our community living out our kingdom convictions together.

Bring a box of donuts to work spontaneously. When coworkers ask you why you did this, say something like "Oh, I have been thinking about you more often these days. I figured this could be a small way of showing it."

FOCUS ON JESUS AND HIS KINGDOM

The goal at this threshold is not to expound a comprehensive systematic theology, answering every little question your friend may (or may not) have. (That's for when someone's actually seeking for answers.) The point here is to help our friends become curious about Jesus, to help provoke an intrigue or an interest in this Jesus guy. As we point to Jesus, we are encouraging people to explore the best evangelist in history. By recounting your favorite Jesus story of the week, you are gently exposing your friends to the Living Word.

When Matthew asked Don more about Jesus and the poor, Don didn't leap on the opportunity to expound the entire gospel and explain clearly what it would mean to become a Christian and ask Matthew if he, that very day, would like to pray the prayer. No. Don had a sense that Matthew was on a very different part of the journey and mostly needed to just become bothered or entranced by Jesus himself. If you ever feel stuck wondering what you could do to help a non-Christian friend grow, telling him or her your favorite stories about Jesus is almost always a great thing to do.

Dousing Curiosity

As we have conversations with curious people, we should be sensitive to what level of interest they actually have. Tuvya Zaretsky, a friend who works with Jews for Jesus, asks a great question: "Would you pour out a whole pitcher of water if all they are holding is a little Dixie cup? No, you would only pour out a few ounces." Tuvya's right. We need to give people what they ask for instead of pouring out everything we know about God the first time they display a Dixie cup's worth of curiosity.

If they have just a thimbleful of curiosity, we could actually douse that small curiosity by answering their small, limited question with a hundred and one apologetic answers we've been waiting to "use" on someone. Try not to dump five gallons of answers on a six-ounce question. Try to assess your friend's curiosity and respond in kind. This approach is much more likely to result in the growth of their curiosity over time.

Now the great thing is, Jesus is very intriguing. No need to try to spice him up. He's as spicy as they come. When folks these days see Jesus himself (rather than clichés or stereotypes about him), they tend to sit up and take notice. People are intrigued by how countercultural

Jesus was, how he embraced the poor and marginalized, how he eviscerated religious hypocrites, and how natural and open he was to those who didn't fit in: the homeless, the prostitutes, the ostracized. They are intrigued by how little he beat around the bush and how often he got to the heart of a person.

People are intrigued by his kingdom, by how focused it is on bringing light into the world, defending the defenseless, embracing the poor and hurting. People love hearing about Christians who move into slums to help set up microenterprises to empower the poor for the long haul. They love hearing about the International Justice Mission, that troupe of Christian lawyers who give up corporate law (and corporate paychecks) to fight against sex slavery.

People are intrigued by the mystery and spirituality and prayer of Jesus' kingdom, how centered it is on experiencing God today through his Spirit. People love hearing about the 24/7 Prayer Movement and stepping into one of these hip, artsy, non-church-looking basements to experience God.

Don: When I was working on my first book *(Jesus with Dirty Feet)* a non-Christian friend of mine asked to read the manuscript. I gave it to him, and while it was lying on his coffee table one of his roommates picked it up and read it.

This guy who picked it up looked about as far from faith as you can imagine: long ago he had dispensed with all religions (especially Christianity), and he had a vibrant life as a militant vegan going (yes, we have militant vegans in Boulder). How could someone be more cynical, more disinterested in Christianity?

But he read the manuscript and had only one question for my

friend: "Did Don get in trouble for writing this?"

It turned out that the Jesus he read about was so interesting, so provocative, so countercultural that he assumed I must have made it all up. He assumed Christians everywhere would be outraged that I had changed Jesus in this way. The thing is, that manuscript was just full of simple stories from the Gospels.

The best thing we can do for our friends at this place in their journey is point them to Jesus and his kingdom. Even though Matthew had all sorts of sophisticated-sounding apologetics questions for Don early on, what he really needed was to care about Jesus. To have his curiosity aroused.

Even though we may want to press other agendas with our friends, it may be that shelving those other issues so that they can take a look at Jesus is the wise move. A friend at church came up to me (Doug) with a question: "Three of my colleagues at work are gay or lesbian. They tell me I am different from other Christians because I am accepting. What should I say to them? I want to tell them that bringing up a daughter with two moms is dangerous. I want to ask them if they think it will negatively affect her development to not have a positive male figure in the home."

My friend was torn between a desire to confront culture and a desire to engage the culture. She was stuck in the tension between being a bold prophet and a patient missionary. In the end I told my friend that instead of pressing that one agenda, she should try to build interest in Jesus. For where her friends were on their journey, this was going to be the wisest move.

CURIOSITY OPENS DOORS

When someone becomes curious about Jesus, it does not make them a Christian. And it does not mean that the hardest part of their journey is over. For many people, the upcoming thresholds will be much more difficult, and they will need even more support and encouragement from the believers in their life.

But moving from complacent to curious is a huge, significant threshold. It opens the door to Jesus, it gets folks staring at him. And what they think of him, after all, is the ultimate question. When the Spirit uses our efforts at provoking curiosity, when God chooses to quicken someone and draw their eyes to him, it opens a door to their relating with Jesus himself. And that is something to celebrate.

When Matthew came back from his summer internship having read the Gospels, he was not a believer. In fact, there was much left to his journey: a growing respect for Jesus and a deep frustration with Christians who didn't seem a lot like him, struggles with Jesus' claims of divinity, a distaste for Christian subcultures, confusion about Scripture, a satisfied contentment with the status of his life, intermittent boredom and even the occasional fistfight.

But eventually, the next spring his journey led to the Boulder Reservoir. It was an early morning, Easter Sunday, and the two of us, Don and Matthew, shivered next to each other in the brisk waters as he was baptized into the kingdom of God.

As glorious as that morning was, we never would have gotten to that place in the journey if Matthew hadn't become curious about Jesus all those months before. It was an essential step on his path to Jesus—and the cold, cold waters of the Boulder Reservoir.

THRESHOLD THREE

Opening Up to Change

"It is clear to me that you have purpose in life and I don't.
What am I missing?"

Abner removed the bong from his closet. "Yeah, that's what I'm talk-ing about!" chirped his party buddies as they got ready to smoke out. Abner crossed the room to find his lighter. To their surprise, though, he proceeded to burn not weed but the bong itself. "What the heck are you doing?" they shouted.

"Sorry, guys," Abner said as he looked over at his buddies. "I'm burn-ing this for God."

That night as Abner burned his bong, he was putting into action that something stirring inside of him: he had become open to change in his life. But how had this beer-drinking, pot-smoking guy become open to change?

During Abner's freshman year he became friends with one of his roommates' buddies, Alex Saulsaido. Their friendship continued into Abner's sophomore year, and it was in this year that things really started to change.

Alex was part of Bruin Christian Fellowship (BCF), the InterVarsity chapter at UCLA. The staff and students in BCF had asked themselves a very dangerous question: "What would we do if we were really serious about trying to reach this entire campus?" The fruit of those discussions was a quarterly outreach event called The Edge. We wanted an event to invite our non-Christian friends to that didn't feel like a typical church service but would provide an atmosphere to talk about spiritual things. We wanted it to be welcoming, and we wanted it to be cool.

So students in the fellowship formed a band and practiced popular songs for hours. The drama team worked on creating modern-day versions of biblical stories. The speaker would pick a recent movie as the topic of discussion and interweave themes from the movie with themes of spiritual growth. It was a cool place to invite our friends to who wouldn't normally set foot in a church or Bible study.

Alex knew that his role in the body was to pray for his friends and invite them to The Edge. So he invited Abner. And as Abner sat in the audience one night and listened to me (Doug) talk about the movie *Face / Off,* he began to say to himself in surprise, *Doug gets it. He understands me.* At the end of the event, Abner filled out a response card, and within a few days he and Alex were sitting in my living room asking me questions.

After we had gone back and forth over spiritual issues for a while, I said, "Can I pray for you right now and help you experience the presence of God?"

Abner said, "No way!"

So I tried another way to nudge him toward God: "God is pursuing you. A famous Christian author once said that God is like the 'Hound of Heaven.' He just can't wait to pour out his love upon you."

The battle in that moment was for Abner's openness. He had come to my apartment for answers, not for changes in his life. What he found was an invitation to change, and that did not feel like good news to him. Would he be open to thinking of God in a whole new way? Would he become open to a new way of looking at life?

Two weeks later Abner and another friend, Mike, went to the track stadium to get high. Under the stars, facing a dark field, Abner continued to think about the things I had said. Questions had been nagging him ever since he went to The Edge. Abner recalls, "With the beer in one hand and the joint in the other, as I was sitting there in the bleachers, I felt like I saw clearly where my life was headed. I was flushing my life away and wasting it just like my uncles had done, and I didn't want to do that."

This clarity shifted things inside Abner. He made up his mind to become open to change. He did not know the path ahead, but he did know that the bong stood in the way. In melting the bong, he was choosing to be open to change in his life. Once he decided to become open to change, it was much easier for Abner to become a seeker and then to come into the kingdom.

THE BEAUTY (AND HORRORS!) OF CHANGE

Abner's story illustrates a principle we have seen again and again in our postmodern friends who have come to faith: before actively seeking God and considering becoming a follower of Jesus, they had to become open to change in their life. And becoming open to change is much harder than it may seem on the surface. It is actually a heroic, mysterious, deep thing.

You see, there's a pretty big difference between just being curious (threshold two) and being open to change. To use a farming analogy: it is as if the ground has been tilled (building trust), the seed has been planted and watered (becoming curious), and now a turning point has been reached: In these ripe conditions, will the seed break through its case and germinate? Will the process of growth take a significant turn?

A heart starting to become open to change is a lot like a little seed's effort to send forth its first shoot. As we continue to water and nurture the process along by building trust and instigating curiosity, the seed begins to sense an environment that is conducive to growth. Many of our friends told us about this pivotal nudge toward growth and change in their lives.

On occasion this environment leads quite naturally and easily to change. As they learn more about Jesus some folks have a hunger for change and grab hold of the moment. Not only do they want to discuss spiritual issues that they are curious about, but they really want good and satisfying answers. Their own lack, their own life, makes them open to considering a new way of life.

But we've found that for every one who easily makes the transition from being curious to becoming open, there are many more who struggle to become open to change or who never do at all but just walk away from the journey to faith altogether.

Out of all five thresholds, becoming genuinely open to change is often the most difficult to overcome. Change is beautiful *and* horrific, after all. (Even for postmodern folks who proudly wave a banner of "openness," being open to real change is a tough thing. Always has been. Always will be.)

Remember the rich young ruler (Mark 10)? This guy wants to hang out with Jesus and follow him around. He seems to have trusted Jesus (threshold one) and came to Jesus with real questions and curiosity (threshold two). He was ready for anything. "Come on, Jesus. Give me your best shot." But when Jesus took it deeper to see if he was open to a real change in his life (in his case rethinking his relationship to money by selling all his possessions and giving everything to the poor), the trusting, curious young man walked away sad. Turns out he was not as open as he thought he was.

Why? Well, he "had much wealth," we're told as a sort of explanation for his behavior. Change has always been hard. So becoming open to change is tricky business. Despite how often and how beautifully openness as a concept is held up and celebrated in our postmodern context, real change is just plain difficult. Becoming open to change is a tough, tough threshold to cross.

One reason this part of the journey is so difficult is that it dawns on our friends that they need to see the world in a new light. Questioning your own worldview and contemplating the Christian perspective for yourself is revolutionary. It can mean coming to terms with deep-seated dissatisfactions and unanswered questions and disappointments. It can mean giving voice to pressing questions that have remained unanswered and purposefully ignored for years: *Where is the drinking taking me? How do the one-night stands feel the morning after? Why isn't the anger and bitterness toward my parents dissipating with time? What meaning might there be in the twinges of guilt after I rip into my roommate?* It can even mean contemplating death and the afterlife.

While becoming open to change opens beautiful doors to healing and redemption and purpose in life, actually opening those doors can feel horrific. It's not surprising that many people resist opening them altogether.

This all points to a very important question: How can we be good friends (and farmers) during this part of our friends' journeys? Is it possible to help people open up to change? Are there ways we can walk alongside our friends as they face the steep, difficult, spiritually charged hill in front of them?

BE PATIENT AS THE JOURNEY UNFOLDS

The need for patience is somewhat obvious. This is deep stuff that sometimes just takes time to unfold. Many of our friends told us how they danced back and forth between wanting change and being terrified and strongly opposed to change. One day they are feeling dissatisfied and are starting to open the door to deep questions and potential life change; the next day they aren't interested in anything except their familiar status quo.

We believers can empathize: how often have we toggled back and forth between embracing a risky call of Jesus and trying to avoid it? This dance takes time, and the process of deciding is often half the point. We need to be patient with our friends in this.

We also need to be patient as they "try on" what it would be like to change. The voice of impatience wants to declare, *This is* true. *You just need to believe. Put aside your questions and accept Jesus.* The voice of patience and compassion invites, *What if this God thing is for real?* Patience gives the gift of space and permission to explore. You offer freedom as you help folks ponder the "what if's." When meeting with Abner, Doug told him to "give God a trial run." This tenuous dance of "suspending disbelief" and daring to try on what it could be like to believe what Jesus says sometimes takes time. And we need to be patient with that.

They need to know that we are their friend regardless of what they decide. They need to know that we like them even as they are, not only if they change. And sometimes they just need space.

Don: Nathan was a friend of mine here in Boulder. We became friends because we were both artists of sorts: I was beginning to dabble in writing, while Nathan was an art major who drew and sketched almost constantly. We started to show each other our "stuff," and since I was mostly writing about Jesus at that time, Nathan became very interested in Jesus and started asking lots of questions about him.

Though Nathan's parents were believers and he had grown up in the church, Nathan had chosen other paths once he came to college and had dismissed Jesus as a sort of boring relic from his childhood. But through our conversations Nathan started exploring Jesus seriously. We were good friends, Jesus was interesting . . . so we got together almost weekly to hang out and talk about Jesus. I assumed Nathan was a seeker, and I treated him like one.

After a few months of this, though, it became apparent that Nathan's surface questions (Why would God send anyone to hell? Can words really have any meaning? Why are Christians so unlike Jesus?) were really a front for deeper questions that he was facing. He knew that following Jesus would affect every area of his life (he had grown up in the church and heard plenty of convicting sermons in his childhood), and yet he really liked his life the way it was.

When I first began to realize this, I felt a bit deceived. Sometimes we can feel tricked by non-Christians: they ask questions that make us think they are true seekers, when the truth is often just that interacting around questions is the easiest, handiest way they know to relate with us. But as I prayed for Nathan, I realized he wasn't trying to trick me— he was genuinely stuck. He didn't know if he wanted to be open to change or not. Some days he did, other days he didn't. That conflict within him was real. He needed real time, and a real Christian friend to walk alongside him during that season of his life. We need to not just endure our friends' journeys but have real patience with them.

Given how deep these struggles are for our friends, as we are patient with them, we also need to be praying our guts out for them. This is spiritual stuff going on here, profound decisions about life and direction and faith. As we consider our own hesitation before a hard deci-

---

Practicing Enduring Prayer

Prayer is essential during this spiritually intense season. There's much going against openness, including very real spiritual enemies. Not only do we need to remember to be practicing intercessory prayer that pushes the battle, but we need to be long-suffering in this.

Read Exodus 17:8-13 and you'll have an image of what we believe is called for. The Israelites are in battle, and whenever Moses raises the Rod of God the battle goes well. Whenever he lowers his arm, though, the battle shifts. So, of course, Moses raises his arm on a hill that's away from the battle. He's interceding.

Seems simple enough. But what happens to Moses? He grows weary. At first his friends bring a rock for him to sit on. But even a seemingly simple activity like holding up your arm while seated becomes fatiguing with time. Eventually Aaron and Hur have to come and help Moses hold up his arm.

We, too, need to intercede for our friends. And we, too, need to be reminded not to stop. Not to grow weary. It might not be a bad idea to get an Aaron and Hur of our own—enlisting other people to uphold us as we uphold others at this spiritually intense time.

---

sion, we realize how key the spiritual side to this step is. This world, our enemy and our fallen nature all conspire against us at this stage of the journey—there are many spiritual influences that would dissuade us from opening the door to change.

Given how many people never make it past this threshold, we can't overstate how our ongoing prayers for our friends need to be redoubled at this part of their journey.

CHALLENGE AS JESUS CHALLENGED

Our friends don't merely need us to be patient and understanding; they also need us to be active as we walk alongside them. This often means tension for us.

If our friend says she's an open person but she is in actuality quite closed to change, how can we help her see this contradiction and escape this common postmodern dilemma? How can we help our friends move toward being open to change in their lives?

Sometimes she will simply need a friend who will say gently, "Don't you want to be open to new things? You told me you think of yourself as an open-minded person." We all know how it helps to have someone come alongside us with encouragement and clarity as we toggle back and forth considering a choice that is scary. We need space to decide. But sometimes we need someone to raise the question for us.

Think about your own life and you'll realize that sometimes we just need to be challenged. Sometimes we need our excuses ignored and our fears pointed out. Sometimes we need someone else to be frustrated by the pains in our life, because we have grown accustomed to the pain ourselves. Sometimes we, as believers, need this kind of help. Is it any surprise that our non-Christian friends would need the same thing?

For most believers, challenging people and appropriately raising the bar for them is probably the most uncomfortable activity to engage in. Most of us have a hard time challenging even other believers—or ourselves!—let alone our non-Christian friends.

The great thing is we have Jesus as a model in this. Jesus challenged people all the time, and though he practiced speaking the truth in love to people wherever he went, his approach differed dramatically depending on where people were and what they needed. We have much to learn from Jesus in this. In three consecutive chapters in John, Jesus challenged people to be open. But in each case his posture toward them, his way of nudging them toward openness, was very different.

Jesus touches the pain of the broken and honest. In John 4 Jesus meets a woman with a past. He wants to help bring her pain out into the open so that he can offer her something categorically better, his own "living water." What is his approach to helping her face her secrets? Gentle affirmation.

When she begins to crack the door on the truth about her brokenness, he honors her several times for her risk of self-disclosure. "You are right," he says to her.

After choosing the path of affirmation, Jesus uses gentle honesty. He puts his finger on her core issue, the whole truth about her. She has been married five times and currently is living with yet another man. She should run from Jesus when this fact is exposed. But she stays—a tribute to Jesus' nonjudgmental truthfulness.

We can, and should, practice the same nonjudgmental truthfulness about our own and other people's brokenness. How do we help people talk about the difficult and disappointing things in their lives? First we ask good questions and listen compassionately. Also, we can speak hon-

estly about our own lives. In fact, our stories of struggle and God's redemption may be the most powerful gift of hope we can offer to those
facing this seemingly insurmountable threshold. Here are some examples of ways the two of us have practiced nonjudgmental truthfulness
while taking a conversation deeper:

- "I'm a mixed bag. I try hard to be loving, but I regularly run out of
  love. I need God to pour it into me again and again. How about you?
  Can you relate? Are you a mixed bag?"

- "We all need help to get by. We might get our fix at Starbucks, at a
  party or on the Internet. But we all need a fix. I find my fix in God.
  What do you think about a spiritual hook-up?"

- "I am tempted to hide the truth about what is really going on inside
  me. To be honest, I prefer façades. But when I am willing to get real
  in front of God and let down my mask, God touches me with his
  love every time. I have learned that everyone is tempted to hide behind a mask. When you are honest with yourself, do you see places
  where you could use the touch of God in your life?"[1]

Jesus mobilized the self-pitying and fearful. In the next chapter of John,
Jesus interacts with a different type of person. This man, a paralytic,
has been stuck by this pool for a long time. In John 5, Jesus does not
honor this man for his truthfulness about his brokenness, as he did in
the preceding chapter. This man does not need to ponder his painful
situation (it really doesn't need highlighting). Instead Jesus calls the
man to do something about it. Jesus doesn't even hesitate, he simply
calls for change: "Get up! Pick up your mat and walk" (v. 8). Jesus

---

[1]For video clips of these kinds of conversations, go to www.ivpress.com and search
for the title of this book.

speaks with authority and doesn't let the man make excuses for himself. He simply says, "Get up!"

Often our friends lack the courage to make life-changing decisions. Satan has them gripped by fear *(What would my friends think? What would my parents think? What about those eight other questions that I haven't found answers to? What if this is a mistake?)*, and what they really need is a nudge to just act. How can we lovingly challenge those paralyzed in fear or guilt? Here are some things the two of us have said to friends:

- "You should ask God for a sign. He loves to give signs to those who are open. How would you feel if God gave you a sign? What is keeping you back?" (Jesus wasn't afraid to give signs to people and help them understand these signs as moments of God's love in their lives. On the flip side, it did upset him when people saw signs yet refused to receive them as gifts from God and respond in faith.)[2]

- "Let me pray with you for ten minutes a day over the next week. If you and I genuinely seek God together for the next seven days, I am confident that he will show up for us. Are you willing?"

- "Remember that story about the good Samaritan? I am going to feed the homeless next week. Please come with me and see how it feels to live out Jesus' words." (Put the Scripture into action. Help them ex-

---

[2]See John 4:48-53. In 4:48, Jesus says, "Unless you people see miraculous signs and wonders, . . . you will never believe." Then he proceeds to give a royal official the sign that he needs in order to believe. Jesus does not fear giving signs as a part of the process of faith. While we can never force God's hand with our prayers, we should have confidence in his character and desire to reveal himself to us. We like to ask boldly for God to reveal himself to our non-Christian friends, because when God does give them the sign they need, we can exhort them to trust God. We have seen many people commit themselves to following Jesus in response. For more on this, read *Get the Word Out* by John Teter.

perience Jesus' words that lead to transformed living and Life itself.)

Jesus agitated the complacent and glib. A couple of chapters earlier, Jesus meets someone who has a lot of good answers about life's hard questions. He has things figured out. In John 3, Nicodemus asks a theological question, "Can a man reenter his mother's womb and be born again?" Nicodemus is a very religious man, but Jesus isn't fooled by his image. He replies, "You are Israel's teacher, ... and do you not understand these things?" (v. 10). In essence: You call yourself spiritual? Jesus uses a little sarcasm here to cut to the chase.

Because of where Nicodemus is coming from, Jesus decides that he needs to be agitated and confronted in love. "Come on now. You should be getting this." Nicodemus likes his old way of viewing the world and his old assumptions about life. He needs someone to jostle him out of his complacency. Sometimes the most loving thing we can do for someone is not to beat around the bush in conversations but instead to just call them on how they are afraid to change.

Our friends who are like Nicodemus tend to be articulate and thoughtful, probably good at debate. It is tempting to enter into their debate mode. Jesus wisely sidestepped the temptation to debate the exact nature of rebirth with Nicodemus. Here are a few ways we've tried to follow that example with our friends:

- "You talk like truth is relative. You tell me that what is true for me is just true for me. But you don't live that way. You live like we all hold things in common. Like love counts for everyone. I'm glad you don't live like a relativist, though you talk like one."

- "You have some interesting thoughts about how life holds together. So how's that working for you? What do you do when life gets hard?"

Soul-Awakening Events

How would you feel if you could invite your curious-but-not-yet-open friends to an event that would help them consider becoming open to spiritual things? These types of preevangelism events can be very helpful in the process of coming to know Jesus. But it is essential to remember that folks at this threshold are not yet seekers. It is better to think of them as skeptics or cynics. With whom are you in relationship? If you know mostly seekers, we would suggest seeker-guiding events (more on these in the next chapter). But if you know mostly cynics, then we suggest events that help the warm-up process.

How would you create an event in order to serve those far from the kingdom? The principles would have to be different from those of seeker events. Based on our experience, we suggest the following:

*1. **Choose relevant topics.** Select topics that they are already thinking about. Movies, pop music and current events are good places to start. Romantic relationships never seem to fade as a relevant topic.*

*2. **Find unique angles.** Surprise them in how you come at these topics. Put yourself in their shoes and come at the topic from their perspective, asking their questions. Jesus always had an unexpected word for those who came to him. Similarly, seek God for an unexpected word for them.*

*3 **Use the arts.** We use music and art and drama because they connect deeply and move souls. The arts are a gift from God, and God can sidestep our skepticism when the arts stir new feelings within us. The soul is supposed to cry out to God, and we can create events that help people get in touch with these yearnings for the living God.*

*4. **Create a safe place.** In contrast to seekers, the not-yet-open often need a place of anonymity. They need to feel safe to explore spiritual things at arm's length, until they warm up to God.*

5. Lead, don't pressure. *These friends need to be led toward God but not pressured. Two mistakes are often made in this regard. On the one hand, we can mistake them for seekers and offer them repeated altar calls. People at this threshold often feel weird about altar calls and can misinterpret them as manipulative or cultish. Swinging to the opposite extreme, we can create environments with no leadership at all. Then those present meander with no help from us at all.*

Jesus connected the dots for the confused and befuddled. In John 5 we see the Jews coming to some really strong and incorrect conclusions about Jesus. They wind up dead set against Jesus (literally) because he has been healing, because he is healing on the sabbath, because he was calling God his own father.

It's interesting that Jesus doesn't try to affirm them and help them see their brokenness and hardness of heart. He doesn't call them to action. And, at least on this occasion, he isn't just provoking them. Instead, he reviews for them everything that has been going on. When Jesus sees how confused they are, he launches into a pretty lengthy overview of events (see John 5:19-47). Jesus talks simply about his relationship to God the Father, he uses the phrase "very truly I tell you" a few times, he outlines what he has been doing, commenting on the fact that they shouldn't have marveled or been surprised. He talks about the Jews—how they sent messengers to John, what they've seen in searching the Scriptures—and he ends by outlining why they are responding as they are and what is going on within them. Jesus just connects the dots for them.

At this threshold we are often simply helping to interpret and connect the dots in our friends' lives. If we truly believe that God has come to seek and save the lost and we trust that he has been at work in their lives already, then it's often a matter of reframing the events and issues in their life within God's story. Gentle confrontation often reveals just how open they are to looking at things from a different perspective. For example, you could say:

• "I don't think these are random events in your life. I think God is pursuing you. I think God is doing all he can to get your attention and win you over."

• "I think God is trying to get your attention through that dream you told me about (or that movie you saw). Your soul is yearning for God, and you should listen to your soul."

It is important to point out, before we move on, that for the most part each of us probably has one preferred way of relating with others. Some of us are very comfortable with gentle truthfulness and empathy. Others really like challenging people to action. As you read about these different postures of Jesus, there was likely one that resonated more with you than the others.

The thing about Jesus is he gave people what they needed. He served people by challenging them in a way that made sense for who they were and where they were. We, too, need to have such a servant heart. What does your friend need in order to be challenged toward openness? In general, we underestimate the importance of our role in speaking words of challenge. If you tend to be that way, please don't let your own comfort level guide how much you speak the truth in love, or you may never get around to it.

To review, we have found that we can help our friends become open by being (prayerfully) patient *and* by challenging them. Both are important.

Don: As Nathan-the-artist and I continued to hang out, we developed a deep friendship. And because I really cared for him, I would sometimes challenge him. In retrospect I am glad I didn't just have patience with Nathan but also honestly confronted him, raised questions and kept pointing him back to Jesus. Eventually Nathan graduated and moved away—and he was still stuck right in the middle of this threshold. He never said yes to considering a life change. In fact, toward the end even his curiosity about Jesus started to wane.

To be honest, it would have been easier to take the either-or track with him. It would have been easier to be the kind friend who simply sits patiently, never bringing up hard questions or challenges. On the flip side, it would have been easier to be the harsh truth-speaker who grills him with intense questions. Though living in the tension was difficult for me, I am glad I took the harder both-and path. Nathan needed both. Being both patient and challenging was a way to serve my friend.

WHAT A THRESHOLD!

To actually see someone cross this threshold is a wonder. Doors of possibility are opened up, they are asking questions about their own life and how that relates to Jesus—it can be exhilarating. But that exhilaration, for some, comes only after great pain and vulnerability and help on the part of their friends.

In the end it is only God's Spirit that is able to overcome the human hesitancy, fear of pain and spiritual enemies that are against someone at threshold three. But when God does this, when he uses our patience and our prayers and our faithfulness to bring someone to a place of being open to change, it is a wonder.

After Abner became open to change, he quickly became a seeker and then a committed follower of Jesus. He told his story to his friends, and God worked in them too. He took significant steps in kingdom leadership. After graduation, he returned to the East Los Angeles neighborhood where he grew up. Instead of using his college education to just get a better life for himself, he has chosen to speak into the lives of countless urban youth, exhorting them to choose life with God instead of gangs, drugs and hopelessness.

God is having an impact on a generation of young Latino leaders through Abner. The Jesus revolution turned him around at age twenty. Now that revolution is being offered to others. Today, I (Doug) count Abner not only as a friend but as an inspiration regarding what God can do in the city.

As you help others through the thresholds of faith, they too may someday become your inspiration when you need it most.

SEEKING AFTER GOD

"I wanted something to happen for me spiritually, but I was waiting for someone to come and show me."

Steve was not a Christian. But over time, Steve observed the life of his Christian friend David from a distance. Steve grew up in urban East Los Angeles. He had friends in gangs. Growing up in East L.A., you survive by being tough, looking hard. Steve worked out all the time. He projected an image of a tough guy.

After a few months, David surprised Steve with an invitation to an event called "Jesus and the Homeless." Steve was intrigued, since he didn't know that Jesus had anything to say about the homeless. When he got there, he was shocked to see Christians sleeping in large cardboard boxes, just as the homeless do. He admired their passion for the poor and oppressed, and he saw that Jesus' words made a real difference in their lifestyle. They didn't fit his stereotype of Christians. Their obedience to Jesus' Word sparked his curiosity.

Another Christian friend invited him to look at the life of Jesus for himself. Since he could see that Jesus had made such a dramatic impact in their lives, it made sense that he could learn something from Jesus. He acted on his curiosity. After about ten weeks of looking together at passages from the Gospels, Steve's Christian friends invited him to join them on a four-day service trip to Mexico, where they would work together building a house for an extremely poor family.

Because of the last ten weeks of looking at the Gospels, Steve knew that Jesus transformed lives. Life transformation became an acceptable concept to Steve, and he even embraced the idea that he himself needed to grow and change.

Then came the trip to Mexico. Each day the team would work on the house, and at night there was a speaker, Matt, who talked about Jesus and his impact on our lives. One evening Matt invited those who wanted to become followers of Jesus to stand and make a commitment. Steve took a risk and stood.

Since Matt knew that follow-up was essential, he had personal conversations with each person who stood. He asked Steve what he was feeling and why he stood during the invitation into the kingdom. Steve answered, "Jesus is cool. You know, I just want to be a better person and do good things."

As they spoke further, Matt sensed that Steve had just become a seeker, not a follower of Jesus. A real commitment had been made, but not the one that Matt had at first assumed. So Matt began to treat Steve like a seeker, someone who had decided to seek out God more purposefully and seriously. Back on campus, he invited him to everything that the Christian community did together—Scripture study, prayer, worship and social events—in order to help Steve come to some conclusions.

A SEEKER ON A QUEST

Those who have recently traveled the path to faith tell us that after trusting a Christian, becoming curious about Jesus and finally being open to change in their life, they still weren't necessarily wanting to come to conclusions. For each of them there was another shift, a fourth threshold, to come: they needed to lean into the journey they were on and decide to purposefully seek final answers, a resolution. They needed to become *seekers*.

Having a friend become a seeker is a delightful part of the journey to faith in Jesus. It is fun and dynamic. We may not notice a big change in their behavior when they switch from just being open to change to actually being a seeker, but to them the internal shift is rather dramatic. Their choice to become a seeker is when the penny drops: "I have some questions that I need answers to. I need to make a decision about Jesus."

There's a subtle but important difference between someone who is sort of meandering toward God and someone who is purposefully seeking out and exploring Jesus. When someone is truly seeking, there is an urgency and purpose to their searching. They feel almost as if it is a quest they are on, and they lean into it with a rather determined posture. Even *they* feel that the time is ripe: they want answers to their questions, they want to come to some conclusions. So they live and ask questions and pray and talk with others to help them resolve the issue.

This is part of how you can tell the difference between a "phantom seeker" and a true spiritual seeker. Phantom seekers do lots of the same things that seekers do: they ask questions, discuss issues, even attend a Bible study or event. But their posture lacks urgency. They have not yet set their mind to walking on a journey toward God, as much as they are open to discussing questions with others. They may be using questions as a way to deflect conversation from something deeper and, perhaps, more vulnerable for them.

True seekers are on a quest. They want to connect dots and come to conclusions. Their questions aren't dodging techniques or casual inquiries; they are genuinely looking for some concrete answers. We have seen three major trends among seekers that distinguish them from phantom seekers or others who may appear on the surface to be seeking.

1. *Seekers seek Jesus, not just God.* There's a difference between merely being spiritually curious (wanting to "connect with the divine") and wanting to know Jesus. Seekers want to know specifically if *Jesus* can be trusted. Can *he* really address my aches of loneliness? Is it *Jesus* who can bring power and hope into my life? Seekers have a clear object of intrigue in their spiritual curiosity. It isn't just about a smorgasbord of religions. They want to know more about this carpenter from Nazareth and how he might be relevant to their life.

2. *Seekers count the costs.* Seekers have been around Jesus, his Word and the Christian community enough to know that there are implications to becoming a believer. It isn't just about "fire insurance," and it's not just about some mental assent to doctrine for absolution. Jesus has some specific advice about how to live, and they feel challenged to believe that this advice is really going to be for their good. "If I become a follower of Jesus, I may need to break up with my boyfriend. We're sleeping together. Do I really want to do that?" Seekers make the implications personal. Jesus doesn't just have general wisdom for a faceless humanity; he has things to say to *me*.

3. *Seekers spend time with Christians.* Because of the trust that has been built with Christians in the community, it is quite normal for seekers to spend a great deal of time with them. They feel included in social and spiritual activities, and on their own initiative they feel comfortable attending Bible studies and church services. They may not feel like

they totally fit in or understand everything that is going on, but they have decided that being uncomfortable at some level is worth it.

While this fourth threshold is subtle (and sometimes is crossed pretty quickly), we have found that it is indeed a unique threshold and that people often need help becoming a true seeker.

Lostness on the far side of this threshold (being open to change but not yet seeking) does not feel like lostness. It *feels* like seeking to them. Those who are now finally open think that their passive posture of receptivity is actually seeking. They are open to the universe, and they often think that is the goal. Openness means arriving.

It is often very helpful to just explicitly challenge them to become a seeker. Tell them that committing oneself to seeking after God is an important decision to make, though it is different from actually deciding to follow Jesus. We've found that folks at this threshold often need to be challenged; otherwise they may stagnate in their path to faith.

In the transition from openness to seeking, a non-Christian decides that they need to make up their mind about becoming a follower of Jesus. So how do you help someone make this subtle shift? How do you help someone go from casually and occasionally asking questions to really being on a quest for answers and for connecting the dots?

LIVE OUT THE KINGDOM OF GOD IN FRONT OF THEM

While some folks do become seekers quite naturally and quickly, others need to see the kingdom lived out in front of them. For many, a view of the kingdom lived out in four dimensions is what catalyzes their posture as a seeker. It helps them seek Jesus, not just God; it helps them count the costs; and it helps them soak in Christian community. In short, it helps them become a seeker.

But it isn't just the "good stuff" that we need to put on display. We need to also open up our struggles and convictions and messy reconciliation. Here are four tangible ways you could start living out the kingdom in front of a friend who may need help becoming a seeker rather than a meanderer.

1. Show them how to build their lives on Jesus' words. Not only did David (and another Christian, Serene) invite Steve to study the Gospels with them, but they studied them with an eye toward how Jesus' words were practical and affected people's lives. Serene studied the house on the rock passage (Matthew 7) with Steve, helping him see how hearing and doing the words of Jesus makes for a solid life. As God speaks to you through your devotions or through a sermon at church, tell your seeker friends how God is challenging or leading you. As you open up your experience, they will come to believe in a God who speaks today. They will expect to build their lives on Jesus' expert advice on practical matters.

2. Open up your prayer life to them. It's not only OK to allow our non-Christian friends to see our "public displays of affection" with God; it's actually quite helpful. Inviting folks into that kind of conversation makes lots more sense when they have seen what praying is like. Various non-Christian friends have come to our prayer meetings and just sit there, eyes wide open, watching us pray. It is a little unnerving, but it is beautiful to let them learn to talk to God by watching us interact with Jesus directly.

Doug: "How do you pray? Can I watch?" I was caught off-guard by the question. I believed in opening up my life of faith to my non-Christian friends, but this was a little intimidating. My friend had recently become open, and he wanted to experience firsthand how I

talked to God and interacted with him daily. So I agreed to have a
quiet time in front of him, praying outwardly what I normally pray in-
wardly. Sometimes I pray through the Lord's Prayer, phrase by
phrase. That day I opened my heart and soul and let my friend experience my intimacy with our heavenly Father.

Serene and Steve had been studying Scripture and eating burgers at
a local In-N-Out restaurant, and Serene prayed at the end of their
lunch. She invited Steve to as well, saying, "Why don't you try praying?" Steve hesitated, but as they left Serene encouraged him, "Just try
talking to God and ask him what you need." So, walking through the
In-N-Out parking lot, Steve tried praying for the first time. Talking
with God and asking him questions is a great thing for those learning
how to seek.

3. *Provide satisfying answers to their initial questions.* If you want to encourage your friends to fully give themselves over to seeking, it's helpful to answer their questions with answers that are actually helpful,
thereby encouraging more seeking. Some non-Christians find abstract,
theoretical, propositional answers to be very helpful. We find that international students from mainland China who are atheists really need
this type of modern reasoning and persuasion. But often our friends
have told us that these "classical apologetics" answers weren't satisfying
for them. They wanted answers that were personal, real and grounded
in real-life experience.

"If God is so good, why is there suffering in the world?" This is an
abstract question, but when your friends ask it they are likely not looking primarily for a philosophically satisfying answer. They may have a
hidden personal tragedy in their own family, or they may not; but ei-

ther way, they secretly yearn to know if you are for real and if your faith makes a real difference in tough situations.

So you *could* quote C. S. Lewis (one of our favorite authors), or you *could* use yourself as a case study of the issue at hand. In that moment, God's work in your personal life is probably the most satisfying answer you can offer them. Talk about suffering *in your own life* and how *you have seen* God's goodness in the midst of that. Answer the question with your life of faith, not with memorized clichés.

By opening yourself and your honest struggles to your friend, you show them the gospel at work. You answer their spoken *and* unspoken questions. And when you do all that, it's easy to ask them how they respond. Honesty on your part catalyzes honesty on their part.

We have created a five-step framework for doing apologetics (answering questions) these days. We suggest that, instead of giving knee-jerk, somewhat abstract answers, you take the conversation up a level, all the way up to the ATTIC:

- *Affirm.* When people pose questions about faith and God, be wildly enthusiastic that they are asking questions. Even if you don't like the particular question they are asking, gush over the fact that they are asking questions. This blesses their curiosity.

- *Translate.* Think about what you would want to say in abstract terms, and then bring that same point down into your own life. Don't quote your pastor, don't talk about what you read in a book. Do the hard work of thinking about that topic in relation to your own journey. Translating is not easy, but it is a great act of love to open your soul for your friend to see.

- *Transparent.* Let your answer be a confessional. Show your friend your struggles. Don't be smug with all the right answers. Let them know you are still a work in progress.

- *Insert yourself as a case study.* "Don't all religions point to the same God?" Instead of answering that abstractly, insert yourself into the question. "Let's look at someone like me as a Hindu, Buddhist, Muslim or follower of Jesus." Using your struggles, look at what each religion says to you and your personal struggles. By personalizing the questions to yourself, you transform the abstract to the real.

- *Challenge.* After answering a question, always bring it back to your friend. "What about you? What are you looking for? Are you a mixed bag like me? Where do you need the touch of a loving God?"

We have found applying ATTIC to be a labor of love. It is like learning a new language. It will come over time with practice. Be patient with yourself. But set your mind to growing in this over time. Your work to provide satisfying answers early on may be just what it takes for your friend to become a seeker.

4. Model seeking. One of the best ways we can encourage seeking in our friends is to model seeking in our own lives. We're not suggesting that believers pretend that they aren't Christians and act as if they were seekers. We're saying that every believer, as they follow Jesus, gets to model exactly what we're talking about here: actively seeking after Jesus. Seeking after Jesus is at the core of who we are as believers. And it can be very helpful to do that seeking *in front of* our friends.

Don: Remember Matthew from the chapter on threshold two? When Matthew came back from his summer internship, he had read all four Gospels and was really, really liking Jesus. But as we continued to meet together I realized that Matthew's questions needed some meaty answers, so I asked him to do a GIG with me.[1] The idea seemed a bit odd to him (he had already read all four Gospels), but he agreed, and so the next time we got together I brought along a passage (John 1) printed out on paper—a copy for him and a copy for me. After chitchatting for a while, I brought the sheets out. I put some pens on the table between us and told him that I like to use highlighters and pens to underline words, write questions, etc., right on the Scripture text itself. This seemed interesting to him, so he agreed to take five minutes on his own to read, mark and write down questions.

We both started reading and writing, but then Matthew stopped and looked at me, obviously puzzled. "What are you doing?" he asked.

"What do you mean?" (I really didn't know what he meant.)

"What are *you* reading it for? I thought you knew all this stuff."

There we were, at an incredible learning moment. I told him how much I love going to Scripture with my thoughts and feelings and questions. I told him what it is like for me to find the voice of Jesus there. I told him how much I love doing that. Matthew looked at me, nodded thoughtfully, and (it seemed to me) went back to his writing

---

[1] When we study Scripture with our non-Christian friends, we call these meetings GIGs (Groups Investigating God). The title communicates that this is a safe place, a place to investigate, to ask our questions. We've found the most effective GIGS are based in the Gospels and are focused on watching what Jesus did or listening to what he said. For further resources on GIGs we suggest checking out InterVarsity Press's GIG series, Becky Pippert's Saltshaker Resources or John Teter's book *Get the Word Out*. Information on all of these resources can be found at www.ivpress.com. For an approach that begins with tough questions people may have, consider Garry Poole's Tough Questions series (Zondervan, 2003).

and reading with even more vigor and purpose than before.

Much more could be said about modeling seeking, but we do want to mention testimonies. There's nothing quite like having believers (especially brand new ones) tell the story of their journey to faith. Sharing our testimonies in this way accomplishes many, many things . . . among them modeling what it looked like for us to begin seeking God with vigor. This kind of modeling is precious and valuable, and celebrates the posture of seeking after God.

In the end, however you can live out the kingdom in front of your friends (showing them how to build a life on Jesus' words, opening your prayer life, providing satisfying answers or modeling seeking) helps them move from meandering to seeking.

CREATE SAFE PLACES FOR PEOPLE TO SEEK

If we want to help people become true seekers, then we should create some safe places for them to do it. When they have the freedom to be honest without fear of being judged or coerced into believing something, they can be vulnerable and allow their internal questions to come out. "Seeker events" can be a very serving tool for our friends who are at this specific threshold, because it allows space for them to assume the seeking posture.

Now, creating a safe environment may sound easy. We used to think it would be easy. But after some failures we have learned some important lessons about creating places for seekers to feel safe—places we like to think of as "frontage roads."

When Doug was learning to drive during high school, he discovered a way to check out the freeway without driving on it. A few blocks from his house there was a frontage road that went parallel to the freeway. He could drive the frontage road at thirty-five miles per hour and, by looking through the chain-link fence over to the freeway, get a very good sense of the freeway traffic.

Many seekers are not yet ready to join the speedy "freeway" of our churches and communities. We are a little too intense for them. But they would love some parallel opportunities to check us out and check out Jesus at half speed so they could really ask all their questions. Whether a seeker event is a weekly GIG, a weekend retreat or a special service designed for large crowds (all of which we use and recommend), we've learned a few important questions to ask before holding such an event. These questions arose from hearing from our friends about what makes such events truly safe.

1. *Is this event designed with real seekers in mind?* One of the interesting things our friends have taught us is that places that seem comfortable to us are often uncomfortable to them. Places that seem natural to us can be confusing and foreign to them. Our language rolls right off our tongues but makes them feel like outsiders—confused and unsafe. So we need to be purposeful and thoughtful about the types of seeker events we create. We always need to start with our seeker friends and their feelings in mind rather than starting with what makes us feel safe or comfortable.

Before moving on from this question, we want to make an important distinction, since we are using words like *seeker* and *event*. Many events are referred to as "seeker events" but aren't really for "seekers" as defined in the five thresholds. Sometimes *seeker* can be taken to mean any non-Christian, and therefore any event held for non-Christians is called a "seeker event."

The reality is that non-Christians can be at very different places, and events for them should be fine-tuned to their needs. For example, The

Edge was designed for people who are skeptics—averse to religion and God—and may not even be curious about spiritual things. It was not, as we are considering the five thresholds, an event primarily geared toward seekers. It was geared toward engaging folks at thresholds one and two, with the goal of helping them grow through threshold three. (Our reasoning for this was rather straightforward: there were very few true seekers at UCLA. So we created an event to reach the core of the campus.)

In Denver, we hold an event called "Smelly Left Sandal," a place for people to come and "take a whiff" of Jesus. It is designed for people stuck at threshold two and is therefore not a seeker event at all. We're not trying to answer final questions, we're trying to arouse initial curiosity. Different events for different purposes.

All of this is just to say, if you are discussing holding a "seeker event" with others, make sure you clarify which threshold(s) you are actually trying to help people step through before planning the event. Make sure you are designing the event for the people you are inviting.

2. Are the expectations clear? Through trial and error, we've found that being vague or not talking explicitly about rules and expectations creates confusion and less safety at "seeker events." People are left wondering how to participate, and their discomfort reduces transparency. The vagueness (though perhaps arising from a loving desire to not pressure people) actually may force people to guard themselves, since they don't know what might be coming or what might be asked of them later on.

Doug: A while ago I was invited to lead a series of GIGs with various curious, open and seeking friends who were connected with our Christian group through different friendships. Sixteen folks showed up for the first GIG to study the Gospel of Mark together. Before beginning the actual study we began by putting a list of our "5 Rules" up on the wall. Yeah, five rules. Here's what they were: (1) You must grow. This is not an academic exercise, but rather we want to be transformed. (2) You must be curious and ask questions. We will go around in a circle to hear everyone's questions. (3) You have to be honest about what is going on inside. You have to share. (4) You have to take risks and try new things. (5) You have to listen to others in the group. No spacing out. Listening and learning is hard work.

To our surprise, the members loved our rules. One woman later joked with us that she had immediately assumed our rules would be more typical—"no swearing, no fighting, no knives," etc. Having clear expectations relieved their unspoken worry: not knowing what would be asked of them or when. And our specific rules also moved them toward seeking. By agreeing to our rules, they were agreeing to look for God and open their souls. Throughout our times together, we regularly invoked one rule or another.

Some of our Christian friends cringe at the idea of communicating group norms. They fear this sounds authoritarian and inauthentic and that non-Christians will run away. Just the opposite is the case: it is surprisingly powerful and important to set clear expectations for people, especially people at this threshold. Of course it is important to be clear about these expectations without being preachy and pushy, but setting explicit expectations early on actually creates clarity and safety for folks and allows the community to be held accountable to grow and to risk. (We also learned that in order for it to be a safe place, we ourselves would have to abide by the same rules!)

3. Is Scripture central to what we've planned? Ultimately, Scripture is where the answers are. Which means people who are wanting to find answers to their questions should have Scripture placed in their hands. While someone is trying to cross threshold one or two it may be too much to ask them to look at Scripture itself (maybe), but at this threshold folks don't need to know *what you think about Jesus* near as much as they need to hear *what the Gospels say about Jesus.*

Unfortunately we've found that seekers are often given "talks" and explanations instead of time to explore the Gospels for themselves. When we explore Scripture with seekers, we try to help them read it as actively as possible. With Matthew, Don used the "manuscript study" method of studying Scripture, which gets folks actively engaging the words and paragraphs themselves.[2] It's often better to walk clear through one Gospel (to let it tell the whole story) than to seek out contextless verses that address a seeker's specific questions. We want people to chew on chunks of Scripture, not just casually lick small pieces of it.

Steve, our friend from the beginning of the chapter, had always assumed that Christianity was a corporate, group-think kind of reality, "like the Borg from *Star Trek.*" This misperception colored how Steve viewed Christianity and Jesus. He was interested in Jesus, but this one question continued to pester him. But one day he was studying the parable of the ten bridesmaids (Matthew 25), and as he studied Jesus' words Steve saw that Jesus wants a unique connection to each person—it's not group-think he's interested in but relating personally and individually to each one. It was by handling Scripture that Steve got this.

---

[2]See chapter 8 in Bob Grahmann's book *Transforming Bible Study* (Downers Grove, Ill.: InterVarsity Press, 2003).

Doug: As the sixteen open-hearted nonbelievers started studying Mark with me, we weren't hearing lectures or clichés about the Christian faith; we were entering together into the world depicted by Mark. Mark became our guide, our teacher and our friend. We learned to love his pictures of Jesus, his terse writing style and his sense of humor. Mark charted the course for this group of open people to become seekers.

In chapter 1, Mark showed us fishermen being utterly transformed by Jesus. We were intrigued by Jesus' impact on them. What is it about Jesus that rocks people's worlds? In chapter 2 he redefined faith. We asked, "How does your definition of faith differ from Mark's?" One person confessed, "Faith is knowing that something is false but believing in it anyway." Mark challenged this definition, showing us a picture of faith that rips off roofs: faith as "determination to get to Jesus." False notions about faith are a major barrier to real faith, and Mark was skillfully dismantling these blocks.

By chapter 4, Mark was pressing us to examine our life choices and priorities. The parable of the sower became a mirror to us of the things we don't like in our lives. And by the time Jesus sent out the disciples two by two, we similarly were ready to take the risk of testifying to what we were seeing of God in our little community.

Scripture is used by the Holy Spirit to speak to people. Not only does it help people face their honest questions but it provides answers. Whenever we hold an event (big or small) for people at this threshold, we are careful to ask ourselves how central the study of Scripture is.

4. Are we guiding seekers or shielding them? Guiding seekers is a form of hospitality: we come alongside our friends as they experience an event and help translate for them what is going on. A guide isn't a know-it-all; a guide helps interpret their experience. This is key for an event to remain safe for our friends. We explain what a Gospel is, we tell them why someone is going to pray during the event, we explain why Christians sing songs.

Seeker guiding is like being a guide at a museum: showing people different rooms and explaining what they are seeing in each room. Shielding seekers is more like changing the content of the museum to be something wholly familiar with the visitors: we take out the explicitly Christian exhibits and fill the museum with stuff they are already used to.

This is the tension between serving folks in thresholds two and three, and guiding seekers. At The Edge (p. 67), we removed worship and prayer to try and help our friends explore faith in the least threatening context possible. But once our friends become seekers, we need to make a switch. To shield seekers from prayer, worship and mission is to potentially misrepresent the life of faith.

At my (Doug's) church, we changed how we introduced worship at our Sunday evening Fusion service (geared toward those in college through those in their thirties). Each week begins with the interpretation: "Worship is when Jesus says, 'Come and see,' and we respond by coming and seeing who Jesus is and what he has for us." This clarity has helped us in two ways. It has helped make worship accessible to our non-Christian friends. And it has shaken the rest of us out of our religious routine, reminding us to actually seek God as we sing. Being "seeker guiding" has made us deeper disciples.

We used to shield seekers from mission. We were afraid of scaring them away by asking them to commit or get involved. Today many of us are seeing the wisdom of inviting non-Christians to engage in kingdom activities, especially ones focused on mercy and justice.

We try to create seeker tracks for all of our service projects and weeklong missions. We also intentionally articulate the gospel to them during these service projects, being explicit about why we serve. (Our acts of service are not self-explanatory. Left to themselves, seekers will come up with their own random explanations. So we need to connect the dots for them.)

One tragic upshot with the rise of the "seeker-sensitive" movement in the 1990s was a grievous polarization between those who wanted "depth" and those doing "seeker sensitive." In many circles, real Christian community and growth in discipleship were supposedly found by isolating your small group and avoiding non-Christians. The thought was that if you welcomed outsiders, you would have to cater to these seekers by watering down your content. It is our great joy to say that you can have *both* depth *and* a welcoming environment for outsiders. Let us embrace the call to courageous leadership to forge communities that do both at the same time.

COMMITTING TO A QUEST

By living out the kingdom in front of our friends and inviting them into safe places where they can stretch their seeking muscles, we can help demystify the seeking process and help them enter the seeking posture.

If the Spirit of God works in the concrete circumstances of someone's life and in the profound depths of their soul, they can cross threshold four: moving from meandering toward Jesus to seeking some final conclusions. And once someone is seeking, only God knows where it might lead.

After coming back from Mexico, Steve went to worship services for the next six weeks. He really enjoyed the new friends and the new experiences he was having; he was safe to seek. And he did. On the sixth week, the topic of the worship service was healing from past pain. Steve came forward to receive prayer from the prayer team during the service. Matt was again the one who prayed for him.

As they prayed, Matt got a sense (perhaps a mixture of intuition and a nudging from the Spirit) that it was time to invite Steve into the kingdom again. He asked a few of Steve's friends to join them, and Matt explained how Jesus invites people into his kingdom and that you have to make a decision to follow Jesus by trusting him with your whole life and joyfully becoming his disciple.

Steve had seen enough. He gladly accepted the invitation and committed his life to Jesus that night! After they finished praying, Matt asked Steve to share what just happened with the people who were lingering nearby after the service. Steve bore witness to God's work in his life. The group exploded in celebration for their new brother in Christ!

Later Steve confided in Matt that he was genuinely relieved that Matt had invited him into the kingdom, because his journey had been just about up. Earlier that same day, Steve had told himself, *I have been exploring Jesus for many weeks. And even though I like these Christians, I am still different. I don't belong. So today is my last day with them. If something doesn't change, I'm not coming to any more events in the future.*

He had been an earnest seeker of Jesus for many weeks. But seeking takes energy and focus. His seeking had run its course. Thank God that Matt took a risk and did not take this seeker for granted.

Entering the Kingdom

"I just had this sense that I couldn't keep this up forever.... I needed to make a decision or just drop the whole thing."

Maité was in her first year of college. She had grown up a Christian but was dead set against evangelism. She could barely even tell people that she was a Christian, let alone talk with others about Jesus.

But during the first months of college, she felt convicted during a Bible study to help out the two women in the dorm room next to hers. These other two first-year students weren't getting along at all and had asked Maité if she'd be willing to move out of her single room and switch with one of them so they wouldn't have to be roommates anymore. Maité liked her single room but felt God strongly urging her to help them out. When she had made the decision to move in with Sarah, one of the two neighbors, an older believer challenged her to be honest with Sarah about why she was doing it.

Telling her new roommate Sarah why she had changed her mind and agreed to switch was a terrifying prospect for Maité. But when Sarah, overjoyed at Maité's decision, pressed her on why she had changed her mind, Maité knew she had to tell her. "My voice shaking, I blubbered, 'Um, well, it's just that . . . see, I kind of feel like . . . the way I see it

. . . honestly Sarah, I think that God told me to move in with you, so I'm going to!'"

Sarah looked at Maité, a bit puzzled, and said, "Well, whatever, I'm just glad you're moving in."

As the school year progressed, Maité began taking small steps to bring Jesus up in conversation, to tell Sarah when she was going to a Bible study. "I started putting two and two together in my mind. Sarah has these struggles, and Jesus has these answers; I knew them both, I should let her in on the goods." One day, when Sarah was in tears over the pressure she was experiencing in school, Maité offered to pray for her, and Sarah welcomed the prayer. Sarah had begun to trust a Christian.

As the spring semester rolled around, the two women had continued to grow as friends. One night, when both of them had gone to bed and the lights were out, their conversation came around to God. Sarah had been reading a New Age book about how everything in your life is connected and there are signs everywhere. Maité knew it was an important moment. "It was pitch-black dark in the room and everything seemed calm, but I felt like my heart was going to pop out of my body, it was pounding so hard. I had this unnerving feeling that God was not going to let me fall asleep until I took this next step and asked her if she wanted to do a GIG with me. So I took a deep breath and asked if she'd be interested in taking a look at what Jesus had to say about some of those things. She answered easily, 'Sure, when can we start?' "

Their GIGs were rich in discussion about Jesus, and both of them told stories of how their lives connected to the texts. Sarah loved learning about Jesus. She soaked in the stories of his character and always wanted to go deeper. She had become curious about Jesus and was open to how his words connected with her own life. So when April rolled around Sarah was more than willing to go with Maité to a weekend retreat called Up Close. The retreat was held on Catalina Island, an hour-long ferry ride from Los Angeles.

The first night they were on the island, Sarah prayed for a sign. She told Maité that the pieces were in place but she couldn't trust that Jesus was someone she could give her life to unless she had some proof. She told Maité bluntly, "I am a science major, so I just need some evidence."

The following morning one of the staff, John, taught out of John 6 where Jesus proclaims, "I am the bread of life. Whoever comes to me will never go hungry, and whoever believes in me will never be thirsty."

Maité remembers the morning, and the rest of the week, very well. "The whole talk was about bread. Bread stories, bread symbolism, bread Scriptures, bread, bread, bread. Halfway through—it hit me. My mind flashed back to our boat ride over to Catalina. Sarah and I had played a word game on the boat. Of all the words in the dictionary, the one that she had picked was . . . *bread.* And because I messed up the game, we randomly got into this long conversation about bread. So as I'm sitting listening to John preach, this connection dawns on me, and I look over at Sarah. Tears are streaming down her cheeks, and she looks at me, smiles and mouths 'bread.' Sarah was amazed that God had given her the sign.

"That night at the evening session John called for those who wanted to come alive like Lazarus to stand, and Sarah went up strong. Unashamed and boldly she stood up for Jesus. I could not contain myself as I sat next to her, trembling with joy. I had never seen such a beautiful thing, and I knew that moment that I'd never be the same. This was even better than when I became a Christian!"

GETTING READY TO PARTY

For all of the friends we've discussed thus far, there came a point where
they needed to make a decision. To repent and decide to follow Jesus.
A point where they wanted in, where they decided to cross a real, eternally significant line. A point where they went from flirting to commitment, where they looked Jesus in the face and said, "I do."

Jesus painted a clear picture of this threshold:

> The kingdom of heaven is like treasure hidden in a field. When a
> man found it, he hid it again, and then in his joy went and sold all
> he had and bought that field.
>
> Again, the kingdom of heaven is like a merchant looking for
> fine pearls. When he found one of great value, he went away and
> sold everything he had and bought it. (Matthew 13:44-46)

The two folks in the parable find treasure. One has been looking intently, seeking for a long time, while the other just stumbles upon the
treasure. But both of them have found it—the treasure that is worth
it all. And once they've found it? Well, then they sell all they have in
order to possess the treasure. Entering the kingdom is just like that: it's
a thing of great joy and great cost. The cost is dear, but is nothing com-
pared with what is being gained.

When our friends want into the kingdom, when they have sought
and sought and see in Jesus what they have always been looking for, they
have a choice: sell all and get it or walk away. To sell all is threshold five.

Jesus regularly nudged people toward this choice. He knew that
seeking isn't meant to go on forever and that people were often served
by his invitation to make a choice. Watch Jesus with Zacchaeus (Luke
19) and you see that Jesus doesn't just walk by him up there in his tree

trying to get a glimpse of the famous rabbi. Instead, Jesus interrupts Zacchaeus's gazing and says, "I want to come and be in your house, I want to interact with you, not just be looked at by you." In Zacchaeus's case, that's all that it took. He entered lunch with Jesus as a seeker. After lunch he was ready to "sell all," turn from his old life and embrace life with Jesus. Conversation with Jesus compelled him across the line. "Salvation has come to this house," Jesus proclaimed as Zacchaeus grasped the treasure set before him.

And when Zacchaeus entered the kingdom, there was a party! This is always the case. Jesus said there is intense rejoicing in heaven when a sinner repents. Witness someone crossing this threshold, as Maité got to do her first year in college, and you will understand just why angels rejoice in heaven whenever it happens.

In Mark 4 (as we saw back in the introduction) Jesus makes it clear that the journey to faith (like the growing of a plant) is mysterious and involves different stages. But even in our postmodern world, we can't forget that there is a definite ending to the parable. "As soon as the grain is ripe, he puts the sickle to it, because the harvest has come" (Mark 4:29). Jesus loved the mystery of the kingdom, and he loved to put in the sickle during his interactions and preaching.

While a truly open-ended, pressure-free process is most needed around thresholds two and three, it isn't as helpful here at threshold five. Letting people just slide casually and vaguely across the line sounds very postmodern-sensitive, but with such a laissez-faire approach we keep people from knowing there is even a line to cross. And we don't help them move from being lost to being redeemed.

In this sense, the fifth threshold resembles various traditional models of evangelism which call for a decision and commitment. The difference for postmodern folks is the significance of each of the previous thresholds. But once they do get to this threshold, they have a very real decision to make, and we can actually help them with it.

BE APPROPRIATELY URGENT

Being a true seeker can't last forever. It's actually quite hard to maintain the posture of seeking, as we saw with Steve in the last chapter. So there is a sort of urgency at this final threshold that is right and appropriate. A decision needs to be made. The ripeness of the fruit deserves our attention and urgency. Every farmer knows this: leave the fruit on the vine too long, and it will spoil.

There is a definite time for "frontage roads" to help seekers gain a safe view of the faith, but the whole reason Doug took the frontage road as a teenager was to see what traffic was like on the freeway so that he could eventually *take an on-ramp* and get onto it. It would be foolish to drive forever on the frontage road, and it turns out it's hard to stay on it for too long. The point is, on-ramps are essential. We need to be sure to provide them from time to time.

Urgency is appropriate desperation for something or someone of great worth. It is diligence; it is goal oriented: *I won't be turned back. We must find this thing or this person!* When we are appropriately urgent, our strategies and actions usually flow intuitively from the situation. Often when our friends have been seeking for some time and we sense that they are ripe and need to make a decision, we can be helpful to them by doing a few simple things:

- Ask them, explicitly and simply, to enter the kingdom.
- If they say no to a call to commitment, ask them why they are saying no. Find out what their questions are, what their blocks are.

- Honestly help them either resolve or set aside the various blocks that are keeping them from choosing Jesus.

- Help them focus on Jesus and the central issues, setting aside non-essential doctrinal issues (resurrection is key, the history of the Crusades is not).

- Help them see how they are responding, or not responding, to Jesus himself.

- Study passages from the Gospels with them that deal with salvation and lostness in honest language.

- Encourage new believers to be telling their stories of journeying to faith, to help seekers see how seeking can end.

- Before asking them to commit, warm them up to the fact that a decision opportunity lies ahead. (For example: "In a few minutes, at the end of my talk, I am going to offer you an opportunity to commit your life to Jesus.")

Some might say that urgency in getting people into the kingdom is manipulative or pushy; we should just let folks meander into the kingdom whenever they please. That sounds nice, but this is not the picture that Jesus paints. Jesus does not want pearl *admirers.* He wants people to sell all and commit themselves to this utterly fantastic pearl. Jesus knew that it is right and natural to sell all to buy the treasure, to pick ripe fruit: "As soon as the grain is ripe, he puts the sickle to it, because the harvest has come" (Mark 4:29).

In Luke 15 Jesus tells us three famous stories of searching for lost things. When the shepherd loses a sheep, he does not sit back and wait for the sheep to find its own way home. This is not the time to revel in the mystery of life and faith. It is the time for a determined, diligent and unceasing search. It is not an option for that sheep to remain lost. The woman who loses a treasured coin is neither casual nor laissez faire. Her mind is set on only one thing: finding her coin. She will not sleep until she finds it. She will not take no for an answer.

The father tirelessly scans the horizon for any sign of a wayward son. His heart breaks. It is both a hopeful and a sad picture. Lost things and lost people make us cry. When the figure of his son does appear on the horizon, we see an Olympic 100-yard-dash effort to reach his son and hug him. No holding back. These are Jesus' pictures of apt urgency.

One problem with seeking is that you get used to it. To seeking, that is. Those who become good at looking for God may get accustomed to always looking, and commitment to anything may feel impossible. It takes a different muscle set to commit yourself after exercising your seeking muscles. Once you commit yourself to Jesus, you are no longer a pearl merchant. That phase of life and identity is gone. You have now become a pearl *adorer*. You are a finder. Those who encourage only the journey often miss the point of the Great Pearl altogether.

Let's use a sports analogy. In football, the last twenty yards on the field have earned a fitting nickname: the Red Zone. Football teams understand that crossing the goal line is where you get the six points, so when you get close, defenses will tighten up and lean against the offense more strongly than at any other point on the field. Because of this (and because of how much football teams want those six points!), teams develop entirely different offensive plays and strategies and formations and plans to use when they get into the Red Zone. There is an appropriate urgency to their plays and an entirely different emotional tenor to their huddles as they strain to get the ball across the line without having to settle for a field goal.

Urgency is not just an OK thing; at times it is downright essential.

Spiritual Warfare

Spiritual warfare is often at a height during these final moments of someone's path to faith, because Satan realizes that he's about to lose his grip on the person's soul as they step into the kingdom of light. In this way threshold five is quite similar to threshold three: the spiritual dynamics are dialed up significantly.

Here in the Red Zone we have found that calling out a "fear of change" and praying through that has helped individuals feel more confident about the step of faith they are about to take.

Acknowledging that there are no guarantees other than the love of God being alive within them helps them understand that they can still have questions.

Practicing enduring prayer (see page 73) becomes important again as we walk alongside folks who are at this threshold.

BE CLEAR, BUT DON'T OVERSIMPLIFY

Our friends stuck at threshold five need a concise summary of what Jesus and his kingdom are all about. They deserve to know, in a nutshell, what Jesus calls people to and what it means to become one of his.

Here we can easily fall into either of two extremes. On the one hand, we can say that the process of trusting Jesus, walking with Jesus and letting him shape our lives is too complex and mysterious to describe simply—and so we just refuse to be clear. Then our non-Christian friends are forced to create their own categories and conclusions regarding what Jesus is really all about. Perhaps they put us and Jesus in their religious box: *Jesus is a smiling guy holding a sheep, looking kind.* They may easily create such a *nice* caricature unless we succinctly help them understand the core truths of Jesus and his kingdom.

On the other hand, we are tempted to oversimplify what's happening. We cheapen everything when we talk about their conversion as if it is all about reciting a short phrase so that they don't go to hell: Just believe in Jesus. Just accept him in your heart. Just ask his forgiveness for your sins. Just read this little pamphlet or look at this little picture. Just recite this little prayer with me.

This is not how Jesus talked about coming to trust him. Jesus talked about people doing a U-turn in their lives. Utter transformation. Selling all to buy the most amazing pearl. Jesus prepared people for a life of following him. If we invite our friends to "just" pray a prayer, how is that helping them follow Jesus wholeheartedly for all their days?

This final threshold, this decision to repent and enter the kingdom, is a part of a much longer process—an intense spiritual, emotional, mysterious process that has been going on over time. There is a sense of urgency, yes. But we can't let that urgency, that desire for our friend to finally cross the line, tempt us into oversimplifying (or reducing) exactly what it means to "cross the goal line." In the short term it may seem easier to sort of "settle for a field goal" rather than to call someone to fully, knowingly and comprehensively enter the kingdom. But this robs them of the intense cost and intense joy of entering the kingdom.

We would be doing our friends a disservice if we ignored the entire process it took for them to get up to the line or if we ignored what is going to happen once they cross the line. We need to be careful to help them connect the dots of their entire process and also help them see what exactly they are saying "I do" to. Following are a few ideas on how to be clear without oversimplifying.

1. The big story. Our good friend James Choung has created a very helpful summary of becoming a Christian specifically written for non-Christians. It is both clear and concise, yet it avoids reducing Jesus to a magic formula. It is the best visual aid we have seen on how to communicate Jesus' kingdom. Check it out![1]

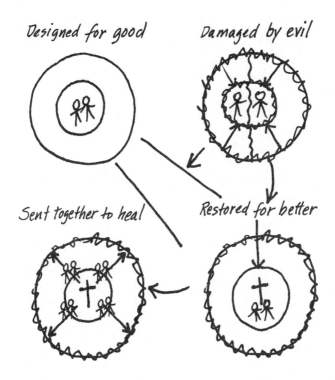

---

[1]*Based on a True Story* by James Choung (Downers Grove, Ill.: InterVarsity Press, 2008) is a short introduction to this helpful diagram. James also has a longer book, *True Story: A Christianity Worth Believing In* (Downers Grove, Ill.: IVP Books, 2008), which places this concise summary of the Christian faith inside a compelling, clarifying story.

2. Wedding vows. Doug's favorite analogy to use when inviting people into the kingdom is wedding vows.[2]

Doug: How would you feel if you came to my wedding and up at the altar this is what I said to my bride? "I commit to loving you several days out of the week. I will give up most of my other girlfriends. I will try hard to be there for you in hard times, but I can't promise anything." The crowd would shout boos at me, right? They would want to walk out! Why? Because my partial vows insinuate that my bride is cheap. She's not worth full vows. I am insulting her. In addition, by making partial vows, I am guaranteeing a weak and unhappy marriage for both of us.

Just as with my wife, we should be indignant if anyone offers Jesus partial vows. Just like Sandy, Jesus deserves full vows. Jesus is not cheap, and he won't be impressed with partial vows.

When I got married, pledging full vows did not mean that Sandy and I had already agreed about every decision we would have to make together for the next fifty years. That's impossible. But it did mean that I would listen to her on every single issue in my life. When we say yes to Jesus, we don't know every decision that lies ahead, but we do know that we will listen to him on every issue in our life.[3]

3. Sports team. Sometimes we use a sports team analogy as we invite people into the kingdom.

---

[2]I (Doug) am indebted to Shannon Lamb, the first person I heard use this analogy to describe entering into relationship with Jesus.

[3]Another thing that is helpful about the marriage and vows analogy is that it can appropriately be extended to the process of first steps toward Jesus (flirting with Jesus), further steps of checking him out seriously (dating Jesus) and then finally crossing the line into his kingdom (pledging marriage vows).

In coming into the kingdom, you are joining a team. Jesus is in charge; he is coach. Expect him to mold you and the team. How much do you need the other players on the team? Utterly. You lean on the team in order to advance and succeed. You expect to work out together and push each other to grow and improve.

4. Revolution. At other times we use the language of revolution:

Jesus is throwing a revolution. Today you have the choice to join his revolution. What is exalted will be humbled, and those who are humbled will be lifted up. If you try to get everyone to serve you, you will be last, but if you chose to serve, you will become great in the kingdom. Jesus' revolution is the most thrilling thing on the globe, and it offers hope to you personally and to all peoples.

Whatever language you use to talk about this final threshold, be sure that it is language that can encapsulate a full sense of your friend's process up to the goal line and the life that awaits them on the other side. Oversimplifying feels like serving, but it actually serves no one.

Talking About Entering the Kingdom

As we talk about entering the kingdom, there are certain phrases and metaphors that come thoughtlessly and easily to our tongues. This is just the nature of language. Phrases create ruts of sorts the more we hear them. If we are not purposefully thoughtful about our language, we will naturally fall into these familiar ruts.

There's a couple of things wrong with these ruts. For one, such phrases tend to be old and dated; they may sound just as awkward and random to our non-Christian friends as any other direct quote from forty years ago would sound. For another, they may not be the best words to use. For example "accept Jesus into your heart" is a

*well-worn phrase that might come easily to your tongue, but
besides not doing justice to the passage it comes from (John 14:23-
24) it can convey a pretty individualistic concept of faith without
much of a sense of Jesus' ongoing role in our lives as our Savior
and Lord—nor does it say anything about the role of the Christian
community.*

*For some of us, learning to be thoughtful about our language will be
like breaking an addiction. Without knowing it, we may have
become addicted to certain phrases. Years ago I (Don) received an
e-mail from someone who had read a book I had written about
Jesus. Our e-mail exchange went something like this:*

> *HER* (after telling me how much she liked what I had written):
> *I just have one more question for you. Have you accepted
> Jesus as your personal Lord and Savior?*
>
> *ME* (after thanking her for her e-mail): *Thanks for your
> question. I have been in the kingdom for 11 years now.*
>
> *HER: I'm glad to hear you've been in the kingdom. (Some
> chitchat.) My one question is: have you accepted Jesus as your
> personal Lord and Savior?*
>
> *ME: Thanks for your question. Yes, I have been a Jesus
> follower for these 11 years.*

*I'd like to say our e-mail exchange ended there. After a few more
rounds, however, I capitulated and used her words. The point is,
there was nothing more biblical about her phrase than there was
about mine, yet she was so addicted to her phrase that using other
(equally biblical) phrases was unthinkable for her. Let's not fall into
these ruts ourselves, as this inevitably leads to us speaking in a way
that sounds either not genuine or just downright confusing.*

When someone crosses this final threshold, they are no longer lost.
They are found. Their eternity has shifted, and the spiritual world ad-

justs to the new reality. As we know from Scripture, God is ultimately the One who calls people to him. Every single person who has ever been found was found because of our great and loving God. The glory goes to him—but we are allowed to be a part of this grand journey and joyful conclusion.

Not only is it humbling to see this happen, but it becomes almost an overwhelming feeling to realize that God has deemed to use you in the process. Your imperfect friendship, your incomplete answers . . . yet here is your friend, now found. Our friend's journey isn't over at this moment (we'll consider life "beyond the thresholds" in the next chapter), but there is nothing like this moment. There is *nothing* like it.

Maité vividly remembers the moment Sarah crossed this threshold:

> After the public time of commitment, Sarah and I went to pray together, and in the most sincere way possible Sarah said to her new Lord, "Jesus, I want you to be my bread of life . . ." When I heard those words I felt like the maid of honor at my best friend's wedding, cherishing each word of her loving vow.
>
> This had come to be the deepest experience of Jesus I'd had in my life up to that point. I had never had more reason and desire to worship than I did then. This Jesus, whom I was seeing so up close, was capable of anything.
>
> At the end of our freshman year Sarah gave me a letter that read, "Maité, thank you for being my bridesmaid. But, more importantly, thank you for introducing me to the true man of my dreams. I feel like I am just in the honeymoon of my marriage, but yet already growing rich in the fact that most of my anxiety, tension, fear and confusion is gone. I know that I can talk to Jesus

about anything. I won't ever forget the divine circumstances that brought you and me together."

LIVING IN THE KINGDOM

"I didn't know what it meant to have Jesus in my life or how that would feel. Now I know—and it's awesome!"

One night during his last year of high school, Russell had an alarming dream. A nightmare, really. He woke up in a cold sweat, the images from the nightmare etched in his memory. In the dream he had died and was sent to hell. He had argued with God—why was *he* being sent to hell? He had always helped people, not hurt people. God just looked him in the eyes and said, "You don't know me." Russell never forgot that dream.

The fall after graduating from high school, Russell got to know some Christians and was impressed at how racially diverse their group of friends was. Their ability to love each other across ethnic lines showed him that they had something unique together, and so he came to a worship service. When they first invited him, the word *worship* brought up mental images of people bowing down to an idol. Instead he saw another weird picture: a bunch of Jesus freaks with their arms in the air, people who were clearly very into Jesus.

After that night one of his new friends, Allen, asked him if he wanted to look at some stories in the Gospels, and Russell agreed.

Now Russell began to know Jesus through Scripture. In November, Russell went to his fourth worship service, and he heard Ana give a talk about the kingdom of God and racial issues. Russell still remembers that night vividly: "Ana spoke about race and ethnicity, and I really related. She was Korean and had always been at a school with Latinos and blacks. I always hated being Chinese American, wishing I was either white or Filipino."

After Ana's talk there were two invitations to respond. The first was for anyone who related to the talk and wanted help with racial healing and ethnic identity. Russell stood up. The second call was for anyone who wanted to commit themselves to Christ. Russell stood again.

He was the only one to stand that night, and everyone started clapping for Russell. It was November 3, 2004.

That night: Russell immediately felt—bad. Here was everyone clapping for him, happy for him. Yet ever since getting to know these people he had been unkind to them. He had treated many of them terribly. He had been obnoxious, and had known it. Their applause and acceptance of him was almost too much that night as he realized what he had been doing and that they had been right about Jesus all along.

The next week: Allen threw a celebration party for Russell. Lots of people came and showered Russell with gifts. They gave him books, tapioca and congratulations on his new life with Jesus. Russell was uncomfortable with the attention.

The first month: Today Russell describes his first few weeks as forty days of being in the desert. "I was the ugliest person, lashing out at people. I had all this hatred and jealousy in me, and it was all coming out. Past moments of being excluded were coming out and needed to be dealt with. I didn't really know how to pray. I would lash out at God, usually late at night. And I was calling friends constantly and asking questions. Why am I feeling this way? Why isn't anger OK? Why did *you* become a Christian? Are you sure he's real?"

The first year: The first year for Russell included some hardships. First there was the flak he got from his friends. One of his closest friends was an atheist. Another good friend was a Jew. An important mentor of his had always bashed Christians whenever he got the chance. At first these folks in Russell's life assumed his conversion wasn't serious. But the longer he kept talking about Jesus, the more they criticized him. One good friend left a comment on his blog: "If you really believe this stuff, I can't associate with you anymore." Russell received harsh instant messages; his friends called him "traitor" and "Bible thumper."

Another hardship in that first year was getting used to Christians and, more specifically, Christian culture. Explicitly Christian words didn't make sense to Russell, and even words like *discernment* and *calling* were used so much that Russell began hating them. The Bible was also confusing. He wasn't used to the vocabulary or structures or names found in it. He was surprised that it wasn't even set up like a normal book—there were columns on each page, for example! Sometimes Russell felt that people were just quoting the Bible at him, and the many Bible references just confused or frustrated him.

THE FIRST YEAR

Once our friends have entered the kingdom, they get to do an amazing thing: they get to live in that kingdom for the rest of their lives on earth. As citizens of this kingdom, we can attest to the exquisite, sublime reality of life within it. We had no idea it was going to be this amazing. And now our friends get to experience that too, for the rest of their lives.

But there's only one first year. And the first year in the kingdom is a unique year. Our friends have told us story after story of their first year: how wonderful it was and, often, the difficulties they faced.

It's not that the blessings of the first year are better than those of every other year (as many of us know, the blessings of the kingdom just keep growing deeper and richer as we continue to follow Jesus). But there's nothing like getting to wake up in this new kingdom, to experience forgiveness, love and truth, *for the first time.* The first year is a tender, wonderful year.

Yet it is also often a very confusing and painful year. It can be painful and confusing because our friends are starting a whole new life. During this first year they will be reexamining many aspects of their life, developing a deeper conscience, figuring out how to live now that they are in this new kingdom.

Being introduced to God's kingdom is like learning one's way around a new country. Here people use strange-sounding words and phrases, and many people engage in unapologetic public displays of affection with God (praying out loud, worshiping enthusiastically) as they are relating intimately with Jesus and his Spirit. Because of all of this it can be a pretty confusing (though also beautiful) season. Jesus said it was like being born all over again.

After entering the kingdom, our friends have dozens of decisions to make about their new life. *How do I live now? How do I relate with my boyfriend now? Do I keep cheating on tests? What about cussing? So what's wrong with porn?* Our friends won't just face questions, they'll face outright opposition. *I can't believe how my old friends are treating me. And I've heard*

Mom telling Grandma that she thinks I'm in a cult! Of course, they'll also face their own doubts and confusions. *I know they said the honeymoon would end one day, but whenever I pray I wonder if there's someone really there or not. Does that mean it was all just an emotional high?*

Heading beyond the thresholds and into the kingdom is a crucial season. Growth is not automatic and must not be taken for granted. Though the seed is planted in the soil, key hazards loom ahead. Jesus knew this and gave us honest warnings about what can go wrong in the growth process after the seed has found soil (Mark 4:1-20).

Jesus said that the sun would climb high and, if the seedling did not have adequate roots, would scorch the young plant. The seedling is in a vulnerable place without strong roots to sustain it.

Jesus talked about weeds too. Every new Jesus follower (just like all of us) will have some weeds in their soil: things that overtly or covertly can choke out their life with God. It may be some hidden aspect of their life that they are not willing to let Jesus speak to. Weeds sap our attention, joy and passion. They deflect us away from Jesus. New believers need to learn to seek God and ask him to point out things that may be twisting their spiritual life.

Yes, going beyond the thresholds is a life of wonder. The first year of that adventure is usually unique in many ways. It is uniquely wonderful and uniquely crucial in the life of a believer. For this reason, it is important that we continue to journey alongside our friends throughout this season.

Once your friend becomes a believer, it is not time to breathe a sigh of relief and go on vacation. We must not abandon our friends once they are across the line. Life with Jesus is neither automatic nor breezy. They desperately need us to help guide them beyond the thresholds.

COMMIT YOURSELF TO THEM

The first practical thing we can do to help a friend move beyond the
thresholds is to commit ourselves to helping them. This may sound obvious, simple and easy. But it really is none of those things.

Consider Ananias, the man God called to help Saul in his first days
as a new believer (Acts 9). The first days of Ananias and Saul's relationship are a great parable or illustration about the commitment it takes
to help a new believer in their new life. [1]

When Ananias is called to go to Saul, it is a hard, hard calling for him
to hear. Saul, after all, was a dangerous, rough, powerful man. Going
to help him was a very scary prospect. Ananias actually debates God a
bit on this point, pointing out what a risky, difficult thing God is asking
him to do.

This is the case for everyone who is called to walk alongside a new
believer. It is a calling that is full of risk. How much time will it take?
Is there any danger? Will they hurt me? Will I have the answers to all
their questions? Will this reveal my own hypocrisies and current sins?
Will I have to confront them and speak blunt truth to them? These are
very real risks that we undertake when choosing to walk alongside a
new believer.

When Ananias gets to Saul, he finds a pretty confused guy. Saul
doesn't understand everything that has happened to him. He's been
groping around blind for days and isn't sure what has happened and
what's going to happen next. "Then Ananias went to the house and en-

---

[1]Ryan Pfeiffer, our good friend in San Diego, pointed us to this passage as a way to
interpret what is happening in the lives of new believers. Ryan and his team have a
thriving new believer ministry at the University of California-San Diego. Many of
the practical insights in this chapter come from Ryan and his community.

Gifts to Help a New Jesus Follower Begin Well

If you know a new believer or are mentoring one, it is a great idea to not overwhelm them with too many Christian books. But you'll do well to get in their hands one or two solid books that will help them pursue their own growth and establish strong foundations for their new life. Not only will they grow from reading a book, but they'll learn how they can be responsible for their own growth.

We suggest titles such as these:

Beginning Well: Christian Conversion & Authentic Transformation *by Gordon T. Smith (Downers Grove, Ill.: InterVarsity Press, 2001)*

Getting Your Feet Dirty: A Down-to-Earth Look at Following Jesus *by Don Everts (Downers Grove, Ill.: InterVarsity Press, 2007)*

My Heart, Christ's Home *by Robert Boyd Munger (Downers Grove, Ill.: InterVarsity Press, 1986)*

Russell says he would give Blue Like Jazz *to a new believer:* Blue Like Jazz: Nonreligious Thoughts on Christian Spirituality *by Donald Miller (Nashville: Thomas Nelson, 2003).*

tered it. Placing his hands on Saul, he said, 'Brother Saul, the Lord—Jesus, who appeared to you on the road as you were coming here—has sent me so that you may see again and be filled with the Holy Spirit.' Immediately, something like scales fell from Saul's eyes, and he could see again. He got up and was baptized, and after taking some food, he regained his strength" (Acts 9:17-19). Saul needed someone to come in and help him interpret what had happened, someone to help him connect the dots, secure what had happened and point a way forward. And this is also what our friends may need.

The challenges of mentoring a new believer often seem harder than they really are, because we weren't braced for them. Once our friend enters the kingdom, we often assume that the hard part is over and let ourselves relax. Actually they need us in this tough part of life as well. It's a season full of many joys and celebrations, but it is also a season of difficult questions, deep confusions and live spiritual warfare.

So what's the first practical step that we advise for helping your friends move beyond the thresholds and further into the kingdom? Commit yourself to walk alongside them. This commitment is a serious thing: they need it. Don't commit yourself to doing it unless you really do have the time, energy and willpower to do this with them.

If you don't, then find someone who does. It is the responsibility of the community to make sure that new believers are mentored closely for the first eight weeks. Don't assume someone will do it. Make sure you know who it is and that they know what they are committing themselves to. New believer ministry is an essential ministry in the church and should be regarded highly.

DO THE FIRST EIGHT WEEKS

If you have committed yourself to walk alongside a new believer, we suggest explicitly setting up a six-to-eight-week intense mentorship with them.

We say six to eight weeks because within that amount of time the first hardships usually hit. If you make a commitment to only three weeks, they may not leave the honeymoon stage or need your help in understanding and responding to hardships during that time.

We say "intense mentorship" because they don't need a class at this stage; they often need someone who knows their life, their friends, their struggles. Someone who is willing to interact with them a few times a week. Someone to pray with them and show them how to pray. Someone to celebrate the new victories. Someone to interpret what's going on, what they're feeling, what they just read. If all people needed was a weekly class, then our first point above (commitment) would be unnecessary. But people don't need just information, especially in these first weeks. They need a mentor.

We say "explicitly setting up" because there are too many dangers involved in being vague at this point. For your own sake and for their sake, we think it is essential to be explicit with them that you are going to have a particular type of relationship for the next eight weeks, after which your relationship will shift some. While intense mentoring and friendship is called for at the beginning, if you aren't clear your friend may think that your friendship is always going to look like this. This thought may either overly excite them (causing them to not develop and find more sustainable sources of support in their local congregation) or freak them out (causing them to think that someone is going to be dropping by and holding their hand for the rest of their life).

In general, there are three phases to this mentorship. The first phase is helping your friends secure their decision. This doesn't mean that their decision or prayer wasn't real and effective; it means that they need their experience interpreted. They need the language to describe what has happened. They need to know how to answer the various doubts that will come and the various emotions that they will feel.

The second phase is the core of the eight-week mentorship. This incubation period is time to help them develop key kingdom habits that will be the foundations they continue to build upon for the rest of their lives.

New Habits Within the First Eight Weeks

As we mentor new believers, it is essential that we help them discover and nurture basic new kingdom habits. There's other ways we will care for them during this period ("giving them fish"), but the most lasting gift we can give them will be helping them develop sustainable habits that they can grow in over time ("teaching them how to fish.")

There are five essential habits that we think should be planted during these first weeks of their new life. These are essential for establishing a strong, healthy root system for new faith. If you are mentoring a new believer, you should find nurturing ways to do these five things:

1. Get them praying. Pray with them; look together at what Jesus taught about prayer.

2 Get them studying Scripture. Look at Scripture together, talk to them about your own joy in Scripture, teach them some basic methods for reading the Bible on their own, orient them to the overall structure, and point them to a couple of passages or books where they can start their reading.

3. Get them connected with community. Introduce them to some folks in your church or fellowship, have some of your mentoring times with someone else present as well, show them what Jesus taught about community and love and forgiveness.

4. Get them to tell their story. Bearing witness to God's work in our lives should be normal from day one. It is so powerful for a new believer to publicly vocalize what they have done; this goes a long way in helping them secure and understand what has happened in their hearts and mind. It also ensures that they will be sharing their new faith with the entire pocket of non-Christians they know— people who may be unknown to your Christian community.

5. Get them serving in some way. It is never too early to begin serving in the body of Jesus. Life in the kingdom is found in serving, washing feet, laying down our lives, so it is essential that early on they begin to learn the joys of serving others: helping out at a service, volunteering with a homeless ministry, tithing and the like.

The final phase is the handoff. After the mentoring period is over, you should carefully guide new believers' transition to a local community, a small group, an attentive friend who will provide long-term sustainable care for them. This doesn't mean you can't continue to disciple them or mentor them or be their friend. It just means that you help them attach more fully to the local congregation as a whole. This will help the health of both of you over the long haul. Ananias's "handoff" of Saul was to the community of disciples at Damascus and later to Barnabas. Aren't we all thankful for the great fruit that came from this smooth transition?

Mentoring is not a guarantee. We can only hope and pray that our investment in new believers will bear fruit over time. Some of those you mentor will break your heart with their choices. Others will grow into people like Mark and Abner, bearing kingdom fruit for the rest of their lives. Every mentoring opportunity is filled with hope and potential. Pray for God to be faithful to continue what he has begun in the new believers you are privileged to mentor.

THE BEGINNING

All of us were at one time lost. And those of us in Jesus can now say that we are found. But this hasn't meant that our life with Jesus, our journey in his kingdom, has ended. We grow more every year, we are pruned by Jesus all the time, we face new struggles along the road.

Just as our moment of conversion wasn't the last word on our faith, so it is with our friends. They have now been born—and can begin living. Let us commit ourselves soberly to not leave our friends once they cross the threshold of the kingdom. Let us help them get their legs beneath them as they begin this new life.

Not only will they be eternally thankful for being a part of their life-saving journey out of lostness, but they will also be tangibly, specifically thankful for all the little mercies we show them in their first year of the rest of their lives.

Russell remembers that year and what was most helpful for him:

It was a tough year. One of the most helpful things for me in making it through this year was honest Christians. It was most definitely not helpful when Christians weren't honest or just responded to every question with a Bible verse. What was more helpful were folks who shared their own stories and were honest about their own struggles.

Walking through an entire Gospel was also huge for me. I was in a study that went all the way through the Gospel of Mark, and even though the study frustrated me at times, in the end it was very, very helpful to learn more about Jesus. I learned about the choices Jesus made and how he treated people.

You know what I'm most thankful for? Ana, who had given me my first Bible, had a tough conversation with me about four months into that year. She knew me well enough to be honest and confront me on my anger and jealousy and how I had been treating everyone. I'm thankful for her boldness.

SERVANT EVANGELISM

We are indebted to our friends and new brothers and sisters for telling us their stories. Each of their journeys to faith has been unique and mysterious, each one a beautiful story of God's intimate pursuit of them. Thank you Mark, Matthew, Abner, Sarah, Russell and the rest of the new brothers and sisters who have shared their journeys (and stories) with us and our communities. Each individual story is a testament to the intimate, personal moving of God within human hearts.

Taken as a whole, these stories illustrate the organic nature of coming to faith, especially the particularly postmodern organic way toward faith. The honesty of our friends is a gift to us. It's a gift because it allows us to be wise farmers—evangelists who are not just zealous and courageous in our witness but also wise in our witness.

Remember Doug's foray into evangelism, standing bravely on his campus singing so that souls might turn and be able to sing the words of that great hymn: "I once was lost but now am found." Doug and his friends were zealous and courageous that day, just not very wise. We offer these thresholds as a wisdom tool, to help us all farm more wisely.

It's not a perfect wisdom tool, of course. There are many exceptions to the five thresholds. People are unique. Your context will change the growth dynamics. Some have said the five thresholds are more cyclical than linear. Maybe that is true. One thing is certain: people will re-gress and "go backward" through the thresholds as often as they progress forward.

We have hundreds of stories of people who once trusted us and then stopped trusting. Friends who were curious, but then their questions dried up, like a hose suddenly turning off. People on the journey who struggled to become open to change, only to slide back into jadedness. And seekers who seemed so close only to end their search without finding Jesus.

These are the stories of heartbreak, when our joy turns to mourning before the Lord. It has happened to us many times, and it will happen to you. We must not allow ourselves to grow cynical when our friends disappoint us. Instead, we ask God for a new heart, his heart for peo-ple, all over again. When our friends stop being curious, we go back to arousing curiosity. When they stop being open, we enter back into the tension of having patience and challenging like Jesus challenged. That is just the way the journey goes.

If the five thresholds framework is not a guaranteed slam-dunk, what is it? We offer it as a discernment tool, something to help you ask good questions. As you seek God for wisdom about what your non-Christian friends need, you are in a great learning posture. Our hope is that as you use this tool with the Lord and your community to un-derstand your non-Christian friends and neighbors more clearly, you will grow in servant evangelism.

We hope that this learning posture will allow you to discard faulty assumptions about conversion that may have been clouding your view of your friends. And we hope that we've provided some practical, tan-gible counsel for how to be more helpful to folks who are at each of the five thresholds, and beyond. It is for these reasons that we have brought the five thresholds out of our communities and into book form.

But in the end, we realize this is not enough. As helpful as this tool may be, it is really not enough.

The reality is we each need to make a decision to serve our non-Christian friends. Just because we understand more clearly what postmodern folks need in their journey, it does not necessarily follow that we will give them what they need. It takes energy and humility and risk to serve others, to allow others' needs to guide our actions. It takes effort and energy to serve our friends, finding out where they are in their journey and stretching ourselves to help them along right where they are.

When it comes to witness, it can be tempting to do it the easy way: to do witness in a way that serves us, is comfortable for us, meets us where we are. It is hard to lead worship out in the middle of a public place, as we did in the opening story. But it is easier to do that once than to patiently befriend those who are far from God. Too often our evangelism plans and efforts are faith filled but don't really help those far from God walk the journey toward Jesus.

A servant evangelist washes the feet of the non-Christian in humility and great empathy, rather than just doing evangelism in a way that the evangelist is most comfortable with. In order to avoid wasting our energy and risks and desperate prayers on self-serving actions, we suggest always asking three simple questions before entering into an evangelistic relationship or event:

1. Who is our audience?

2. What do they need at this stage in their journey?

3. How can we help them take the next step toward Jesus?

Even with the greatest, most insightful and relevant wisdom tools, we each still have a decision to make in witness: will we put our friends' needs before ours, or will we do what we want?

In Jesus, may we all serve by laying down our own lives (and preferences and expertise and habits) and washing the feet of our wonderful postmodern friends and neighbors. This is our prayer for ourselves, and for you.